Love on every plate

Mediterranean Lifestyle Cookbook for Beginners with 1500 days of Recipes for health & happiness + 21 day meal plan

Becca Russell

TABLE OF CONTENTS

TABLE OF CONTENTS

TABLE OF CONTENTS

CHAPTER 3
SIDE DISHES

CHAPTER 4
APPETIZERS, SNACKS, AND SALADS 93

INTRODUCTION

I. A short history of a revolutionary discovery

Mediterranean Diet is an umbrella term for the eating habits of the people from the countries surrounding the Mediterranean basin: Italy, Spain, Greece, Cyprus, Turkey, parts of the Middle East, and the coast of North Africa.

But it is not widely known that in fact, the popularity of this particular dietary pattern across the world is due to a prominent epidemiologist and nutritionist from the University of Minnesota: **Ancel Keys**.

It all started back in 1944.

Ancel was an American soldier who landed at Paestum by Salerno as part of the Fifth Army. He was there to free Italy from Nazis and Fascists.

But fate also had another task in store for him.

His instincts as a scientist were piqued by the peculiar eating habits of the locals.

All their meals were rich in fruits and vegetables, coupled with grains and legumes. Occasionally they consumed fresh fish, dairy products, eggs, or cheese – but in moderate amounts.

What amazed him most, however, was that they would eat very little red meat.

That is the exact opposite of the standard American diet, which has always glorified the myth of red meat consumption.

After the War, Ancel decided to move to Italy and specifically to Pollica, a small village in the province of Salerno, Campania.

And he lived there for 28 years.

There, he had the opportunity to closely investigate the effects of nutrition on the health of the local population.

He was the first scholar to scientifically prove a **direct link between the particular type of diet followed by people in the Mediterranean, and low rates of cardiovascular disease**.

The result of his work is the "Seven Countries Study" which started in 1958 and is a cornerstone of nutritional science to this day.

The study compares the diets of seven countries: the United States, Italy, Finland, Greece, Yugoslavia, the Netherlands, and Japan.

The findings are unmistakable: the more the diets of the countries studied deviate from the Mediterranean diet, the greater the incidence of cardiovascular disease.

The "Seven Countries Study" publicized a revolutionary discovery worldwide: heart health and the prevention of other serious diseases start with a particular kind of diet.

Since then, the latter has become known as the "Mediterranean Diet".

Fast forward to the present day, when it has received hugely important recognition.

On November 16, 2010, UNESCO decided to include the Mediterranean Diet in the *List of Intangible Cultural Heritage of Humanity*.

II. The best diet for the heart

Today, Keys' findings are confirmed by the most important American health institutes.

The Mediterranean Diet is recommended by the **American Heart Association** because it is beneficial to prevent heart disease and stroke.

In fact, it reduces the risk of the onset of all those factors that are related to coronary heart disease: obesity. It actually reduces the likelihood of all the factors that are linked to coronary heart disease: obesity, diabetes, high cholesterol, and high blood pressure.

Not all diets – including some very popular ones, such as paleo, ketogenic, Atkins, and others – are approved by the AHA. Quite the contrary. Some have long been proven harmful to the heart.

1. "Good" fats vs. "bad" fats

Even the **Mayo clinic** has endorsed the Mediterranean Diet, explaining in an article what features make this type of diet the top ally of the heart.

To begin with, **people who follow the Mediterranean Diet tend to replace foods rich in harmful fats with healthy ones**.

Wait a minute... Rewind... Do you mean there are healthy fats?

Yes, indeed!

Granted, when it comes to nutrition, everyone points the finger at fats. *"Fats: you are the number one enemy of public health!"*

But this is an oversimplification that doesn't match up with reality.

Fats – or lipids, to use their scientific term –

are vital elements for the proper functioning of the body.

For one thing, it would be really hard to get up, walk, go to work, or run if we didn't eat fats.

That's because fats – along with carbohydrates – provide us with the fuel to live on.

But that's not all: they also convey vitamins and minerals to where they are needed. Indeed, vitamins are fat-soluble – which means that we can only absorb them when they are dissolved in fat.

Finally, they are key building blocks of cells and tissues.

Well then, so what fats are bad for you?

We have come to learn that **we need to distinguish between "bad" fats (so-called saturated fats) and "good" fats (also known as unsaturated fats).**

"Bad" fats – that we must be very wary of – lurk in butter, lard, dairy products, red meat, deep-fried foods, and virtually all processed foods.

These are really "bad" because they tend to increase our blood cholesterol levels. And high levels of cholesterol can cause fatty deposits to form in the blood vessels. The consequences of which can be lethal: heart attack and stroke.

Imagine if your mechanic used crappy oil for your car's engine, instead of the one recommended by the manufacturer.

After a few miles, you'd find yourself stranded on foot in the thick of rush-hour traffic. Engine dead, car good for nothing but the scrapyard.

What happened? Quite simply, the cheap oil left behind some residue of grime and deposits that accumulated over time.

… Until eventually, the oil itself can no longer flow through and act as a lubricant for the metal parts of the engine, causing them to break.

This is exactly what happens to our arteries.

And unfortunately, *"heart disease is the leading cause of death for men, women, and people of most racial and ethnic groups in the United States".*

So, if we don't want something irreparable to happen to our "engine," we must promptly replace "bad" fats with "good" fats.

Unsaturated or "good" fats – the kind that is useful for our bodies and lowers the killer cholesterol – **just happen to be present in the main staples of the Mediterranean Diet.**

In vegetable oils, for example – most notably olive oil.

But also in nuts (walnuts, almonds, hazelnuts, cashews, Brazil nuts, pine nuts, pistachios, etc.) and seeds (sesame, flax, chia, sunflower, etcetera).

Fish such as mackerel, herring, sardines, tuna, and salmon, are also rich in omega-3 fatty acids, the best friends of the heart.

Omega-3 fatty acids help reduce triglycerides, abate blood clotting, and decrease the risk of stroke and heart failure.

In essence, the Mediterranean diet replaces saturated fats (the enemies of the heart), with unsaturated fats (its allies).

Grilled chicken instead of fried chicken, brown rice instead of refined flour, olive oil instead of butter… Simple, right?

2. The 4 superpowers of the Mediterranean Diet

A 2013 study conducted by **John Hopkins** researchers provided striking results in favor of the Mediterranean Diet.

Mediterranean-style nutrition – combined with not smoking, daily exercise, and a healthy weight – reduces the risk of death from heart disease and stroke by 80%.

In particular, the Mediterranean Diet has 4 super beneficial effects that help our body stay healthy and energized:

- **BENEFIT #1:** It keeps "bad" cholesterol levels low (basically, unsaturated fats clean blood vessels from waste, instead of clogging them as saturated fats do)
- **BENEFIT #2:** It helps the body to regulate blood sugar levels, therefore preventing the onset of diabetes.
- **BENEFIT #3**: It keeps harmful inflammation at bay.
- Inflammation is the natural response of our immune system to viruses or bacteria. But if such inflammation becomes chronic – a common condition in overweight people – our body is damaged.
- **BENEFIT #4:** It enables our arteries to stay flexible and prevents the buildup of plaque, which is a major contributing factor to heart attack or stroke.

3. The Diet that brings a smile to your face

But there is another unexpected benefit discovered by researchers at the Sydney University of Technology.

In a research study, they divided a panel of 72 young people aged 18-25 into two groups. One group began to follow the Mediterranean diet, while the other stuck to a normal diet.

At the end of the survey period, the ones who had been following the Mediterranean diet scored higher on the Beck's Depression Inventory (BDI) scale than the others. A higher score means a better mental condition.

Could it be that food also affects mood?

Let's see how. According to Michael D. Gershon, director of the Department of Anatomy and Biology at Columbia University, **the intestine is our "second brain"**.

Indeed, in our intestines, there is a network of 500 million neurons.

And it is estimated that 90% of serotonin – otherwise known as the "feel-good hormone" because it is responsible for us feeling happy – is produced in the intestines.

Strange as it may seem, simply put it means that **our happiness depends more on our guts than on our brains**.

Fine, but what does that have to do with the Mediterranean Diet?

A diet rich in fiber (which is found in legumes, fruits, and vegetables) is **particularly helpful in maintaining a balanced bacterial flora**, a key factor in determining the health and proper functioning of the gut.

4. Lose weight while you eat

The Mediterranean Diet is not a fixed program – it is customizable and easy to follow.

It does not ban fats but replaces them with "healthy" ones.

It does not forbid carbohydrates but replaces them with wholegrain ones.

Zero deprivation and zero guilt.

And the amazing thing is that-as studies in the *American Journal of Medicine* show - **despite its differences from "conventional" diets, it still helps with weight loss**.

This is because the underlying principles for controlling weight gain are the same as those of the Mediterranean Diet, namely:

- Avoid refined grains
- Avoid added sugars
- Avoid fats from processed foods (junk food).

A 2016 study by the *American Journal of Medicine* found that a sample of people who followed the Mediterranean diet lost between 9 and 22 pounds after a year, compared to those with a low-carb diet, who lost only between 6 and 11 pounds.

5. The Best Diet 2022 according to U.S. News

The Mediterranean Diet ranked first in the **Best Diets Overall 2022** ranking by U.S. News & World Report.

The ranking consists of 40 diets selected from 27 experts in nutrition, obesity, nutritional psychology, cardiovascular disease, and diabetes.

The 40 Diets are rated based on seven criteria:

1. Ease in following the diet
2. Ability to lose weight in the short term
3. Ability to lose weight in the long term
4. Nutritional completeness
5. Safety
6. Ability to prevent diabetes
7. Ability to prevent heart disease

The mean score of these 7 factors decided that the absolute best diet in 2022 is the Mediterranean Diet.

III. Mediterranean Diet 101

After discussing its history and scientific evidence, it's now time to understand **how the Mediterranean Diet works**, so that we can

implement it in our daily lives.

In fact, all you need to do is follow a few simple rules that are very clearly illustrated by a diagram known as the **Mediterranean diet pyramid.**

Created in 1993 by the nonprofit organization Oldways in collaboration with the Harvard School of Public Health and WHO, it provides a priceless guideline.

The foods at the basis of the pyramid are those that are consumed at each meal and in greater quantities, while at the top of the pyramid there are foods that are eaten very rarely.

A rectangle at the base of the pyramid represents the importance – besides nutrition – of staying active.

1. The 5 foods that should always be on your table

If you follow the Mediterranean Diet, these are the foods you should eat daily:

1. **Vegetables** - e.g. tomatoes, broccoli, cabbage, spinach, onions, cauliflower, carrots, Brussels sprouts, cucumbers, potatoes, sweet potatoes, and turnips.
2. **Fruit** - apples, bananas, oranges, pears, strawberries, grapes, dates, figs, melons, peaches
3. **Nuts and oily seeds** - almonds, walnuts, macadamia nuts, hazelnuts, cashews, sunflower seeds, pumpkin seeds. You can also eat almond butter and peanut butter
4. **Whole grains** - oats, brown rice, rye, barley, corn, buckwheat, bread, and whole-wheat pasta
5. **Legumes** - beans, peas, lentils, peanuts, chickpeas.

Legumes may be replaced for a few meals a week with animal proteins.

DIET TIP: The recommended daily servings are 3 portions of unrefined grains and 5 portions of seasonal fruits and vegetables.

2. The 4 foods you can eat in moderation

In the Mediterranean Diet, protein comes mainly from legumes, which can be consumed daily. The diet can be supplemented with animal protein, although its consumption should not be daily:

1. **Fish and seafood** - salmon, sardines, trout, tuna, mackerel, prawns, oysters, clams, crab, mussels
2. **Dairy products** - milk, cheese, yogurt
3. **Eggs**
4. **Read meat** – beef, pork

DIET TIP: In the Mediterranean Diet, it is recommended to eat 1 or 2 servings of fish and seafood per week. Dairy products, eggs, and white meat should be consumed weekly in moderation. As for red meat, very rarely.

3. The 6 foods you should avoid if you want to stay healthy

Refined sugars are at the tip of the Mediterranean Diet "Pyramid". This means that they are the kind of food that should be consumed less often than anything else.

Let's see why.

When we eat something sweet, it raises the level of sugars in our blood (blood sugar) – to which our body reacts by producing insulin.

The result is that there is a spike in instant energy, followed shortly thereafter by a sudden drop that triggers a craving for more.

The more you eat sugar, the more you crave it.

But the energy of refined sugars has very few nutrients. Basically, we assume a lot of calories that need to be disposed of, but are "empty".

So much so, that the paradox of obese people is that they are "undernourished" and often lack essential nutrients for the body.

But sugars are not only found in sweets.

Here is a list of foods not recommended if you want to follow the Mediterranean Diet:

1. **Added sugars** - soda drinks, candy, ice cream, white sugar, syrups, baked goods
2. **Refined cereals** - white bread, pasta, tortillas, chips, crackers
3. **Trans fats** - are found in margarine, deep-fried foods, and many processed foods
4. **Refined oils** - soybean oil, canola oil, cottonseed oil, grape seed oil
5. **Preserved meat** - cold cuts, sausages, hot dogs, cold cuts, dried meat
6. **Highly processed foods** - fast food, ready meals, microwaveable popcorn, cereal bars.

DIET TIP: *Sugars should be avoided because they are addictive and can make you fat.*

4. Red Wine

Now to a controversial subject. Typically alcohol is one of the first items banned from weight-loss diets because of its sugar content.

The Mediterranean Diet, on the other hand, permits drinking moderate amounts of red wine.

Indeed, wine contains polyphenols – natural antioxidants that may have beneficial cardiovascular effects.

So you can enjoy the benefit and pleasure of a good glass of red wine with your meal after a hard day's work!

DIET TIP: *In the Mediterranean Diet, moderate intake of red wine is allowed – but no more than two glasses for men, and one for women, per day*

IV. The 4 golden rules for a new and healthier lifestyle

The Mediterranean Diet allows us to radically change our lifestyle without much effort, and certainly no fasting or sacrifice when it comes to taste and enjoyment of food. All we need to do is apply 4 golden rules.

RULE #1: Stay active

Fundamental to the Mediterranean way of life there is healthy physical activity.

That doesn't mean we need to sign up for Pentathlon training tomorrow; nor need we train as Navy Seals.

Just take the stairs instead of pushing the elevator button, take the dog out, go for a walk outdoors, a bike ride with children or friends, a swim, a ride on the treadmill…

A good plan would be to do this for 30 minutes a day, 5 days a week.

Unwilling to walk? Here are **5 good reasons to go for a walk:**

1. It's good for the mood
2. It unlocks ideas
3. It helps you shed excess pounds in less time
4. It allows you to better regulate your blood sugar by greatly reducing your risk

of diabetes, as confirmed by the American Diabetes Association

5. It promotes digestion.

RULE #2: Food is about sharing

Have you ever seen an American blockbuster set in ancient Rome? Usually, at some point, there's a banquet scene. We see Roman nobles busy enjoying food and drink while they converse amiably.

This is an effective depiction of one of the most important values for the Mediterranean society: **considering meals as a moment of sharing**.

A value whose significance has been recognized by UNESCO.

Food around the Mediterranean is about using all of your senses. Use your (clean) fingers to select the best lettuce leaves and smell the tomatoes before slicing them to make a nice salad.

Turn off the TV and sit at the table in good company.

In addition to spending more joyful and carefree time with your loved ones, you will also find that food tastes better.

Taking time to chat with your partner, telling each other about your day over a glass of red wine, while preparing or eating a nice dinner... it's enough to reduce all the stress accumulated during the day!

... Not to mention the fact that if you learn to cook tasty and colorful Mediterranean dishes, your family and friends will love you!

RULE #3: Eat in season and rediscover the taste of food

When you start following a Mediterranean Diet, your palate needs to get used to enjoying natural food.

It's not difficult! Keep in mind that food-wise, the Mediterranean countries, for ex-

ample Italy, are renowned for being among the best places in the world.

Would you like to know what their secret is?

Well, there are two of them. The first one is **eating seasonal fruits and vegetables**.

For example, there's a considerable difference between a seasonal fruit – preferably grown locally – and a fruit grown in a greenhouse.

The first one is much tastier. Not to mention the fact that seasonal and local fruit is often cheaper.

The second one is **learning to utilize the incredibly rich selection of super flavorful herbs and spices**: garlic, basil, mint, rosemary, sage, nutmeg, cinnamon, pepper...

RULE #4: Use olive oil

Olive oil is the **main condiment in the Mediterranean Diet**.

It enriches each dish with its incredible flavor.

It's from olive oil that we get the largest amount of unsaturated fats ("the good guys") that help lower blood cholesterol levels.

It's also rich in Omega-3s, the heart's best friends.

But that's not all.

It protects our skin from aging because it contains vitamin E – a powerful antioxidant to counteract free radicals.

DIET TIP: Adopt the Mediterranean Diet first and foremost to feel better. It is NOT at all about restrictive eating, guilt or sacrifice. Weight loss comes as a result of eating healthily and adding simple exercise that helps blood sugar and digestion.

▍V. 3 simple steps to get started

Initially, changing habits always involves a small effort.

For starters, you need some basic organization – deciding what to eat beforehand, minimizing prepping times, and having everything you need at your fingertips.

As for the rest, just follow these 4 simple steps.

STEP 1. Go grocery shopping.

Here's what your shopping list should look like:

- Olive oil
- Fresh fruits and vegetables (best); frozen as an alternative
- Legumes
- Herbs
- Whole grains - oatmeal, quinoa, whole-wheat pasta, and brown rice
- Nuts, seeds, and nut butter
- Fish – you may also buy it frozen or canned
- White meat
- Eggs
- Dairy products
- ...and to round it off, a nice bottle of red wine (to drink in moderation!)

STEP 2. Choose high-quality olive oil

It's easy to say olive oil - but when you are standing in front of a supermarket shelf, you are confronted with so many of them. Which one to choose?

The first thing to know is that the best olive oil is **extra virgin olive oil (EVOO)**.

Here are **3 tips** to make sure you choose a **top-quality EVOO**:

- Read the label and make sure it states that the oil is cold-pressed extra virgin olive oil
- Read the origin of the oil, and the type of olive used
- Read the harvest or bottling date to make sure the oil is as fresh as possible.

STEP 3. Follow the 21-day meal plan

Now let's get started!

In this book, we have devised a 21-day meal plan that includes everything you need.

Easy and fast to follow, it is the best way to start introducing healthier eating habits and more energy, well-being, strength, and vitality into our lives.

VI. The truth about the Mediterranean Diet: 10 mistaken beliefs

1. The true Mediterranean diet exists only in its original countries

The Mediterranean Diet can be adopted wherever there are plentiful fruit and vegetables, whole grains, legumes, and animal proteins.

2. The peoples of the Mediterranean eat all in the same way

Truth is, there is not one single Mediterranean Diet. For example, an Italian does not eat like a Greek. The term *Mediterranean Diet* simply represents common food principles.

3. People living in Mediterranean countries are all thin and healthy

The actual eating habits of today's Mediterranean peoples retain only a few aspects of the Mediterranean Diet of yesteryear. Indeed, in these countries, the consumption of sugars and red meat has increased considerably, with a subsequent increase in heart disease.

4. The Mediterranean diet is expensive

The staple foods of the Mediterranean Diet are affordable for almost any budget. Additionally, if you only eat seasonal vegetables – perhaps locally sourced – the savings are often considerable.

5. The Mediterranean diet is not suitable for working people

Just plan in advance what you are going to eat, and make sure you have all you need in your fridge. The book features many recipes that are easy and quick to prepare.

6. If I often eat out, I can't follow the Mediterranean diet

Just remember to always order a salad and replace bread and pasta with whole-grain alternatives if possible.

7. In the Mediterranean diet, you can drink all the wine you want because it's good for the heart

Drinking red wine is indeed recommended, but in limited quantities: two glasses a day for men, one for women.

8. In the Mediterranean Diet, you can eat a lot of cheese

The intake of dairy products is recommended in moderate portions and 2-3 times a week at most.

9. In the Mediterranean Diet, you can eat all the pasta, pizza, and bread you want

Carbohydrates can be eaten but only in the recommended amounts and should be replaced with whole-grain ones. For example, spelt, barley, rye, etc.

• In the Mediterranean, diet you can eat all the sweets you want

Quite the opposite: refined sugars should be avoided or consumed very occasionally. The golden rule is to replace dessert with fruit – preferably in-season varieties.

VII. Conclusions

As we have seen, the Mediterranean Diet is one of the <u>healthiest</u> diets in the world – and by far the best diet for the heart.

It's not a strict diet, and you don't have to count calories or weigh food.

Just stick to the few simple rules we have already discussed:

- engage in moderate physical activity daily
- eat lots of fruit and vegetables, nuts, seeds, and legumes
- replace refined carbohydrates with wholegrain ones
- eat fish, eggs, dairy products, and white meat, but not every day
- avoid red meat, refined sugars, and processed foods
- enjoy a nice glass of red wine with your dinner if you like!

Now that you've learned the basics, there are no excuses!

It's time for us to dive headfirst into the Mediterranean cuisine through recipes that are easy to prepare and delicious too.

Chapter 1
Breakfast Recipes

Walnut & Date Smoothie

10 minutes

10 Minutes

2

Ingredients

- 4 dates, pitted
- 1/2 cup of milk
- 2 cups of Greek yogurt, plain
- 1/2 cup of walnuts
- 1/2 teaspoon cinnamon, ground
- 1/2 teaspoon vanilla extract, pure
- 2-3 ice cubes

Directions

1. Blend everything together until smooth, and then serve chilled.

Nutrition: Calories: 257; Protein: 15.3 g; Fats: 18.5 g; Carbohydrates: 7.5 g

Strawberry Rhubarb Smoothie

10 minutes

8 minutes

1

Ingredients

- 1 cup of strawberries, fresh & sliced
- 1 rhubarb stalk, chopped
- 2 tablespoons of honey, raw
- 3 ice cubes
- 1/8 teaspoon ground cinnamon
- 1/2 cup of Greek yogurt, plain

Directions

1. Start by filling a small saucepan with water. Bring it to a boil over high heat, and then add your rhubarb. Boil for three minutes before draining and transferring it to a blender.
2. In your blender add yogurt, honey, cinnamon, and strawberries. Blend until smooth, and then add your ice.
3. Blend until it becomes thick with no lumps. Enjoy cold.

Nutrition: Calories: 252; Protein: 8.5 g; Fats: 6.2 g; Carbohydrates: 41.3 g

Gingerbread & Pumpkin Smoothie

10 minutes

1 h 5 Minutes

1

Ingredients

- 1 cup of almond milk, unsweetened
- 2 teaspoons of chia seeds
- 1 banana
- 1/2 cup of pumpkin puree, canned
- 1/4 teaspoon ginger, ground
- 1/4 teaspoon cinnamon, ground
- 1/8 teaspoon nutmeg, ground

Directions

1. Start by mixing your chia seeds and almond milk in a bowl. Allow them to soak for at least an hour, but you can soak them overnight.
2. Transfer them to a blender.
3. Add your remaining ingredients, and then blend until smooth. Serve chilled.

Nutrition: Calories: 224; Fats: 8.5 g; Carbohydrates: 33.3 g; Protein: 3.7 g

---

The Great Barley Porridge

5 minutes

25 minutes

4

Ingredients

- 1 cup of barley
- 1 cup of wheat berries
- 2 cups of unsweetened almond milk
- 2 cups of water
- 1/2 cup of blueberries
- 1/2 cup of pomegranate seeds
- 1/2 cup of hazelnuts, toasted and chopped
- 1/4 cup of honey

Directions

1. Take a medium saucepan and add it over medium-high heat.
2. Add barley, almond milk, wheat berries, and water and bring to a boil.
3. Reduce the heat to low and simmer for 25 minutes.
4. Divide amongst serving bowls and top each serving with 2 tablespoons of blueberries, 2 tablespoons of pomegranate seeds, 2 tablespoons of hazelnuts, and 1 tablespoon of honey.
5. Serve and enjoy!

Nutrition: Calories: 337.4; Fats: 6.4 g; Carbohydrates: 62.8 g; Protein: 7.3 g

Cardamom-Cinnamon Overnight Oats

10 minutes

0 minutes

2

Ingredients

- 1/2 cup of vanilla, unsweetened almond milk
- 1/2 cup of rolled oats
- 2 tablespoons of sliced almonds
- 2 tablespoons of simple sugar liquid sweetener
- 1 teaspoon chia seeds
- 1/4 teaspoon ground cardamom
- 1/4 teaspoon ground cinnamon

Directions

1. In a mason jar, combine the almond milk, oats, almonds, liquid sweetener, chia seeds, cardamom, and cinnamon and shake well.
2. Store in the refrigerator for 8 to 24 hours, then serve cold or heated.

Nutrition: Calories: 158; Fats: 6.5 g; Carbohydrates: 20.3 g; Protein: 4.5 g

Vanilla Raspberry Overnight Oats

10 minutes

0 minutes

2

Ingredients

- 2/3 cup of vanilla flavour unsweetened almond milk
- 1/3 cup of rolled oats
- 1/4 cup of raspberries
- 1 teaspoon honey
- 1/4 teaspoon turmeric
- 1/8 teaspoon ground cinnamon
- Pinch ground cloves

Directions

1. In a mason jar, combine the almond milk, oats, raspberries, honey, turmeric, cinnamon, and cloves and shake well.
2. Store in the refrigerator for 8 to 24 hours, then serve cold or heated.

Nutrition: Calories: 81; Fats: 1.3 g; Carbohydrates: 16.2 g; Protein: 1.8 g

Baked Dandelion Toast

10 minutes

15 minutes

4

Ingredients

- 2 tablespoons of olive oil
- 1 small red onion, thinly sliced
- 1/8 teaspoon of red pepper flakes
- 2 tablespoons of lemon juice
- 1 bunch of dandelion greens
- 1/4 teaspoon of salt
- 1/4 teaspoon of pepper
- 4 ounces of feta cheese
- 1/4 cup of plain yogurt (not Greek)
- 1 teaspoon of grated lemon zest
- 1 loaf ciabatta, split and toasted
- 2 tablespoons of small mint leaves

Directions

1. Heat olive oil in a large skillet over medium heat. Add red onion and red pepper flakes and cook, occasionally stirring, until softened, 4 to 5 minutes.
2. Add lemon juice and cook until evaporated, about 30 seconds.
3. Remove from the heat, add dandelion greens (about 8 oz, with 5 inches of stem discarded), season with salt and pepper, and toss until it starts to wilt.
4. Meanwhile, crumble feta cheese into a mini food processor and pulse four times. While the food processor is running, add yogurt and then the lemon zest; puree until smooth and creamy. (You can also crumble feta very finely into a bowl and beat with yogurt and lemon zest.)
5. Spread over ciabatta, cover with greens, and sprinkle with mint.

Nutrition: Calories: 148; Fats: 9.7 g; Carbohydrates: 8.5 g; Protein: 6.9 g

Orange French Toast

5 minutes

15 minutes

6

Ingredients

- 1 cup of unsweetened almond milk
- 3 large eggs
- 2 teaspoons of grated orange zest
- 1 teaspoon vanilla extract
- 1/4 teaspoon ground cardamom
- 1/4 teaspoon ground cinnamon
- 1 loaf of boule bread, sliced 1-inch thick (gluten-free works well)
- 1 banana, sliced
- 1/4 cup of berry and honey compote

Directions

1. Heat a large nonstick sauté pan or skillet on a medium-high heat.
2. In a large, shallow dish, mix the milk, eggs, orange zest, vanilla, cardamom, and cinnamon.
3. Working in batches, soak the bread slices in the egg mixture and then place them in the hot pan.
4. Cook for 5 minutes on each side, until golden brown. Serve, topped with banana and drizzled with honey compote.

Nutrition: Calories: 109; Fats: 2.8 g; Carbohydrates: 17.3 g; Protein: 5.1 g

Cool Tomato and Dill Frittata

5 minutes

10 minutes

4

Ingredients

- 2 tablespoons of olive oil
- 1 medium onion, chopped
- 1 teaspoon garlic, minced
- 2 medium tomatoes, chopped
- 6 large eggs
- 1/2 cup of half and half
- 1/2 cup of feta cheese, crumbled
- 1/4 cup of dill weed
- Salt as needed
- Ground black pepper as needed

Directions

1. Pre-heat your oven to a temperature of 400 degrees F.
2. Take a large-sized ovenproof pan and heat up your olive oil over medium-high heat.
3. Toss in the onion, garlic, and tomatoes, and stir fry them for 4 minutes.
4. While they are being cooked, take a bowl and beat together your eggs, half and half cream, and season the mix with some pepper and salt.
5. Pour the mixture into the pan with your vegetables and top it with crumbled feta cheese and dill weed.
6. Cover it with the lid and let it cook for 3 minutes.
7. Put your pan into the oven and let it bake for 10 minutes.
8. Serve hot.

Nutrition: Calories: 140; Fats: 9.8 g; Carbohydrates: 4.3 g; Protein: 9.7 g

Zucchini Muffins

15 minutes

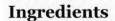

15 minutes

4

Ingredients

- 4 organic eggs
- 1/4 cup of water
- 1/2 teaspoon organic baking powder
- 1 and 1/2 cup of zucchini, grated
- 1 tablespoon fresh thyme, finely chopped
- 1/4 cup of cheddar cheese, grated
- 1/4 cup of unsalted butter, melted
- 1/3 cup of coconut flour
- 1/4 teaspoon salt
- 1/2 cup of parmesan cheese, shredded
- 1 tablespoon fresh oregano, finely chopped

Directions

1. Preheat the oven to 400 degrees F.
2. Lightly grease 8 cups of a muffin tin.
3. In a bowl, add the eggs, butter, and water and beat until well combined.
4. Add the flour, baking powder, and salt and mix well.
5. Add the remaining ingredients except for the cheddar and mix until just combined. Divide the mixture evenly between the prepared muffin cups and top with cheddar.
6. Bake for about 13-15 minutes or until the tops become golden brown. Remove the muffin tin from the oven and leave it to cool on a wire rack for about 10 minutes.
7. Carefully tip the muffins out onto a platter and serve warm.

Nutrition: Calories: 107; Carbohydrates: 3.9 g; Protein: 7.8 g; Fats: 6.6 g

Cheesy Egg Muffins

20 minutes

10 minutes

6

Ingredients

- 4 eggs, large
- 2 tablespoons of Greek yogurt, full Fats:
- 3 tablespoons of almond flour
- 1/4 teaspoon baking powder
- 1 and 1/2 cup of cheddar cheese, grated

Directions

1. Preheat your oven to 375 degrees F. Add yogurt, and eggs to a medium bowl, season with salt, and pepper, and then whisk to combine.
2. Add your baking powder and coconut flour, then mix to form a smooth batter. Finally, add your cheese, and fold to combine.
3. Pour your mixture evenly into 6 silicone muffin cups and set to bake in your preheated oven.
4. Allow them to bake until the eggs have fully set and are lightly golden on top, about 20 minutes, turning the tray at the halfway point.
5. Remove the muffins from the oven. Allow them to cool on a cooling rack and then serve. Enjoy.

Nutrition: Calories: 107; Carbohydrates: 1.7 g; Protein: 8.3 g; Fats: 7.9 g

Quick Spinach & Egg Bake

10 minutes

25 minutes

12

Ingredients

- 10 eggs
- 2 cups of spinach, chopped
- 1/4 teaspoon garlic powder
- 1/4 teaspoon onion powder
- 1/2 teaspoon dried basil
- 1 1/2 cup of parmesan cheese, grated
- Salt

Directions

1. Preheat the oven to 400 degrees F. Grease the muffin tin and set aside.
2. In a large bowl, whisk eggs with basil, garlic powder, onion powder, and salt.
3. Add cheese and spinach and stir well.
4. Pour egg mixture into the prepared muffin tin and bake for 15 minutes.
5. Serve and enjoy.

Nutrition: Calories: 83; Fats: 5.4 g; Carbohydrates: 1.2 g; Protein: 7.5 g

Caprese Omelet

10 minutes

10 minutes

4

Ingredients

- 6 eggs, beaten
- 2 tablespoons of olive oil
- 3 and 1/2 ounces of cherry tomatoes, halved
- 1 tablespoon basil, dried
- 5 (1/3) ounces of mozzarella cheese, diced

Directions

1. Whisk basil into the eggs, and lightly season. Set a large skillet with oil over medium heat.
2. Once hot, add tomatoes and cook while stirring.
3. Top with egg and continue cooking until the tops have started to firm up.
4. Add cheese, switch your heat to low, and allow it to fully set before serving. Enjoy!

Nutrition: Calories: 215; Carbohydrates: 3.1 g; Protein: 29.4 g; Fats: 16.2 g

Yogurt Chicken Breasts

10 minutes

10 minutes

4

Ingredients

YOGURT SAUCE:
- 1/2 cup of plain Greek yogurt
- 2 tablespoons of water
- Pinch saffron (3 or 4 threads)
- 3 garlic cloves, minced
- 1/2 onion, chopped
- 2 tablespoons of chopped fresh cilantro
- Juice of 1/2 lemon
- 1/2 teaspoon salt
- 1 pound (454 g) of boneless, skinless chicken breasts, cut into 2-inch strips
- 1 tablespoon extra-virgin olive oil

Directions

1. Make the yogurt sauce: Add the yogurt, water, saffron, garlic, onion, cilantro, lemon juice, and salt in a blender, and pulse until completely mixed.
2. Transfer the yogurt sauce to a large bowl, along with the chicken strips. Toss to coat well.
3. Cover with plastic wrap and marinate in the refrigerator for at least 1 hour, or overnight.
4. When ready to cook, heat the olive oil in a large skillet over medium heat.
5. Add the chicken strips to the skillet, discarding any excess marinade. Cook each side for 5 minutes, or until cooked through.
6. Let the chicken cool for 5 minutes before serving.
7. Tips: If saffron isn't available, you can use 1/2 teaspoon of turmeric instead. To make this a complete meal, serve it with your favorite salad or cooked brown rice.

Nutrition: Calories: 178; Fats: 6.8 g; Carbohydrates: 20.5 g; Protein: 27.3 g

Toasted Sesame Ginger Chicken

10 minutes

15 minutes

4

Ingredients

- 1 tablespoon toasted sesame ginger seasoning (or toasted sesame seeds, garlic, onion powder, red pepper, ground ginger, salt, pepper, and lemon)
- 1 1/2 pound of boneless, skinless chicken breast
- 4 teaspoons of olive oil

Directions

1. Put the chicken breasts on a clean, dry cutting board.
2. Gently flatten the chicken breasts to the approx. thickness of 3/8 using a beef hammer or the back of a frying pan.
3. Dust with some seasoning.
4. Heat the olive oil over a medium-high flame in a big, nonstick frying pan.
5. Add the chicken and cook on one side for about 7-8 minutes, until a beautiful crust has been created—it will be mildly orange.
6. Gently turn the chicken and cook on the other side for a further 5-6 minutes before the chicken is thoroughly cooked.
7. Serve hot or cooled with your favorite side dish. Makes about 4 servings.

Nutrition: Calories: 136; Fats: 5.9 g; Carbohydrates: 0.6 g; Protein: 21.6 g

Coconut Tender Chicken Bites

10 minutes

15 to 20 minutes

6

Ingredients

- 4 chicken breasts, each cut lengthwise into 3 strips
- 1/2 teaspoon salt
- 1/4 teaspoon freshly ground black pepper
- 1/2 cup of coconut flour
- 2 eggs
- 2 tablespoons of unsweetened plain almond milk
- 1 cup of unsweetened coconut flakes

Directions

1. Preheat the oven to 400 degrees F. Line a baking sheet with parchment paper.
2. On a clean work surface, season the chicken with salt and pepper.
3. In a small bowl, add the coconut flour. In a separate bowl, whisk the eggs with almond milk until smooth.
4. Spread the coconut flakes on a plate. One at a time, roll the chicken strips in the coconut flour, then soak them in the egg mixture, shaking off any excess. Finally place them in the coconut flakes to coat.
5. Arrange the coated chicken pieces on the baking sheet. Bake in the preheated oven for 15 to 20 minutes, flipping the chicken halfway through, or until the chicken is golden brown and cooked through.
6. Remove from the oven and serve on plates.

Nutrition: Calories: 147; Fats: 3.6 g; Carbohydrates: 8.3 g; Protein: 20.3 g

Tender and Tasty Fish

15 minutes

15 minutes

4

Ingredients

- 2 teaspoons of olive oil or oil
- 1 Tablespoon cumin, garlic, cilantro, red pepper, onion, parsley, paprika, salt & pepper mixed seasoning
- 1 3/4 pounds of cod or haddock (wild-caught)

Directions

1. Clean your fish and slice it into 1" pieces.
2. Sprinkle with the seasoning and toss to coat the fish thoroughly.
3. Heat the olive oil over a medium-high flame in a big, nonstick frying pan.
4. Add the fish and cook for about 10 to 12 minutes until the fish is transparent and splits into pieces. Be cautious not to overcook; otherwise, the fish may be dry and chewy.
5. Makes about 4 servings.

Nutrition: Calories: 126; Fats: 3.2 g; Carbohydrates: 0.6 g; Protein: 23.8 g

Charred Sirloin with Creamy Horseradish Sauce

5 minutes

15 minutes

4

Ingredients

- 1-3 tablespoons of horseradish (from the jar)
- 6 tablespoons of low-fat sour cream
- Sprinkle of salt, pepper, garlic and onion powder to taste
- 1 1/2 pound of sirloin steaks, trimmed & visible fat removed

Directions

1. Preheat the grill to a medium-high temperature.
2. Season the steak on all sides.
3. Place on the grill and cook on either side for about 5-7 minutes, depending on how thin the steak is and how you like your beef.
4. When the meat is cooked, mix the sour cream and horseradish to make the sauce. To thin the mixture to produce a sauce, add water, one teaspoon at a time. Put aside until required.
5. Let the meat sit for five minutes on a chopping board, then slice thinly.

Nutrition: Calories: 374; Fats: 27.4 g; Carbohydrates: 1.6 g; Protein: 31.4 g

Beef Hash with Zucchini

19

10 minutes

20 minutes

2

Ingredients

- 1 sliced small onion
- 6 to 8 medium sliced mushrooms
- 2 cups of grass-fed ground beef
- 1 pinch of salt
- 1 pinch of ground black pepper
- 1/2 teaspoon smoked paprika
- 2 lightly beaten eggs
- 1 small, diced avocado
- 1 ounce parsley

Directions

1. Preheat your air fryer to a temperature of about 350 degrees F. Spray your air fryer pan with a little melted coconut oil.
2. Add onions, mushrooms, salt, and pepper to the pan. Add the ground beef and the smoked paprika and crack in the eggs.
3. Gently whisk your mixture, then add the pan in your Air Fryer and lock the lid. Set the timer to about 18 to 20 minutes and the temperature to about 375 degrees F.
4. When the timer beeps, turn off your Air Fryer, then remove the pan.
5. Serve and enjoy your breakfast with chopped parsley and diced avocado.

Nutrition: Calories: 351; Protein: 28.3 g; Fats: 21.8 g; Carbohydrates: 12.5 g

Sausage Stuffed Mushrooms

20

5 minutes

25 minutes

4

Ingredients

- 4 large Portobello mushrooms (caps and stems)
- 1 capful (1 Tablespoon) Garlic & Spring Onion Seasoning or chopped garlic, chopped chives, garlic powder, onion powder, salt, and pepper to taste
- 1 1/2 pound of lean Italian sausage (85-94% lean)

Directions

1. Preheat the oven to 350 degrees F. Clean the mushroom stems.
2. Chop the stems into tiny pieces and place in a bowl. Put the meat and spices into the bowl and mix all the spices well, using your fingertips. Set the smooth side of the mushroom caps on a wide cookie sheet or baking tray.
3. Divide 4 equal sections of the meat mixture and lightly press one section into each mushroom head.
4. Bake for about 25 minutes & serve crispy. Make 4 servings.

Nutrition: Calories: 211; Fats: 14.8 g; Carbohydrates: 0.8 g; Protein: 19.6 g

Chargrilled Mediterranean Vegetable and Beef Lasagna

25 minutes

55 minutes

4

Ingredients

- 1 tablespoon of butter
- 1 tablespoon of olive oil
- 100 g diced onion
- 2 garlic cloves
- 500 g ground beef
- 3 tablespoons of tomato paste
- 400 g of diced tomatoes
- 100 ml of hot water
- 1 cube of beef stock
- 1 bay leaf
- 1 teaspoon of basil
- 1 teaspoon of oregano
- 80 g Parmesan or Grana Padano cheese
- 1 tablespoon of butter (for the sauce)
- 50 g of Parmesan or Grana Padano cheese (for the top)
- Dried lasagna sheets
- 500 g of grilled Mediterranean vegetables

Directions

1. Preheat the oven to 360 degrees F and lightly grease a 1.2-liter frying pan.
2. Heat the oil and butter in a large skillet or saucepan over medium heat and gently fry the onions until they thaw and soften.
3. Add the ground beef and season with salt and pepper. Fry until completely brown.
4. Stir in the tomato paste and cook for a few more minutes. Add the canned tomatoes, herbs, stock cube, and hot water mix well, reduce the temperature and simmer over medium heat for about 10 minutes.
5. For the sauce, heat the butter in a medium saucepan until it starts to bubble slightly. Stir in the flour and cook, constantly stirring, for one minute.
6. Remove from the heat, whisk in the milk until combined, and return to the heat.
7. Stir occasionally as the mixture thickens. When the mixture has thickened, remove from the heat and stir in 80 grams of cheese. Put aside.
8. Before assembling, add a spoonful of sauce to the bottom of an oven dish. Finish with a layer of dried lasagna sheets. Spoon the remaining beef mixture over the pasta and drizzle with some cheese.
9. Add another layer of lasagna sheets and top with the grilled Mediterranean vegetables. Finish with more lasagna sheets. Spoon the cheese sauce over until the last layer of pasta is completely covered.
10. Sprinkle with the remaining cheese and bake in the oven for 35-40 minutes, or until the top is golden and bubbly.

Nutrition: Calories: 569; Fats: 30.8 g; Carbohydrates: 32.8 g; Protein: 40.2 g

Spaghetti Pesto Cake

10 minutes

40 minutes

6

Ingredients

- 12 ounces of ricotta
- 1 cup of Basil Pesto, or store-bought
- 2 tablespoons of olive oil
- 1/4 cup of freshly grated Parmesan cheese
- Salt
- 1 pound of spaghetti

Directions

1. Preheat the oven to 400 degrees F. Set a large pot of salted water to boil over high heat.
2. In a food processor, combine the ricotta and basil pesto. Purée into a smooth cream and transfer to a large bowl. Set aside.
3. Coat a 10-cup Bundt-type pan with olive oil and sprinkle the Parmesan cheese. Set aside.
4. Once the water is boiling, add the pasta to the pot and cook for about 6 minutes until al dente.
5. Drain the pasta well and add it to the pesto cream. Mix well until all the pasta is saturated with the sauce.
6. Spoon the pasta into the prepared pan, pressing to ensure it is tightly packed. Bake for 30 minutes.
7. Put a flat serving platter on top of the cake pan. Quickly and carefully tip the pasta cake upside down. Gently remove the pan. Cut into slices and serve topped with your favorite sauce, if desired.

Nutrition: Calories: 380; Fats: 10.8 g; Carbohydrates: 58.3 g; Protein: 12.5 g

Italian Pork Loin

15 minutes

2 hours & 20 minutes

4

Ingredients

- 1 1/2 pound of trimmed pork loin
- 1 teaspoon of salt
- 3 garlic cloves crushed and peeled garlic
- 2 tablespoons of extra-virgin olive oil
- 2 tablespoons of fresh rosemary, chopped
- 1 tablespoon lemon zest, freshly grated
- 3/4 cup of dry vermouth (or substitute with white wine)
- 2 tablespoons of white wine vinegar

Directions

1. Preheat the oven to 375 degrees F
2. Tie the loin with kitchen string on two sides and the middle so it will not flatten.
3. Mash salt and garlic to make a paste. Stir in the other ingredients except for the vermouth and the vinegar. Rub the mixture all over the loin and refrigerate without covering for an hour.
4. Roast the loin, turning it over once or twice for 40 to 50 minutes. Move it onto a chopping board and let it cool for 10 minutes.
5. While cooling, pour the vermouth and vinegar into your roasting pan over a medium-high temperature. Simmer for 2 to 4 minutes, scraping off the brown bits and reducing the liquid to half.
6. Remove string and slice the roast. Add excess juice to the sauce and serve.

Nutrition: Calories: 273; Carbohydrates: 0.8 g; Fats: 15.3 g; Protein: 32.6 g

Grilled Skirt Steak

15 minutes

8-9 minutes

4

Ingredients

- 2 teaspoons of fresh ginger, finely grated
- 2 teaspoons of fresh lime zest, finely grated
- 1/4 cup of coconut sugar
- 2 teaspoons of fish sauce
- 2 tablespoons of fresh lime juice
- 1/2 cup of coconut milk
- 1-pound beef skirt steak, trimmed and cut into 4-inch slices lengthwise
- Salt, to taste

Directions

1. In a sizable sealable bag, mix together all ingredients except steak and salt.
2. Add steak and coat generously with marinade.
3. Seal the bag and refrigerate to marinate for about 4-12 hours.
4. Preheat the grill to high heat. Grease the grill grate.
5. Remove steak from the refrigerator and discard the marinade.
6. With a paper towel, dry the steak and sprinkle with salt evenly.
7. Cook the steak for approximately 31/2 minutes.
8. Flip the steak and cook for around 21/2-5 minutes or until it is as done as you desire.
9. Remove from the grill pan and keep to one side for approximately 5 minutes before slicing.
10. With a sharp knife, cut into desired slices, and serve.

Nutrition: Calories: 223; Fats: 7.1 g; Carbohydrates: 12.4 g; Protein: 27.6 g

Festive Season Stuffed Tenderloin

15 minutes

60 minutes

8

Ingredients

- 4 teaspoons of olive oil
- 2 minced shallots
- 1 8-ounce pack of sliced cremini mushrooms
- 3 minced garlic cloves
- 1 tablespoon of fresh thyme, chopped (add extra for garnish)
- 1 1/2 teaspoons of fresh parsley, chopped (add extra for garnish)
- 1/4 cup of dry sherry (or you can use red wine vinegar)
- 32 to 40 ounces of beef tenderloin
- 1/2 cup of bread crumbs, fresh whole-wheat
- 1 teaspoon of salt
- 1/2 teaspoon of black pepper

Directions

1. Preheat your oven to 425 degrees F.
2. Warm 2 tablespoons of oil on medium heat and cook shallots for 5 minutes or until tender. Add mushrooms and stir-cook until they soften (about 8 minutes).
3. Mix in the garlic plus herbs and cook for a minute more before adding the dry sherry. Reduce the sherry by half, then remove and let it cool.
4. Cut the beef lengthwise resembling butterfly wings. Cover with plastic and pound using a mallet until 1/2-inch thick.
5. Stir breadcrumbs into your mushroom mixture before spreading evenly onto the beef. Leave a 1-inch space around the edge.
6. Roll the beef jellyroll style and secure with kitchen string at one-inch intervals. Place the rolled meat on a rack inside a shallow roasting pan.
7. Mix the rest of the fixings and rub over the beef—roast beef for 35-40 minutes for medium-rare or according to your taste.
8. Allow the beef to cool for 15-20 minutes with loosely tented foil before carving. Serve with extra thyme and parsley.

Nutrition: Calories: 165; Carbohydrates: 5.9 g; Fats: 9.2 g; Protein: 14.4 g

Pasta Bolognese

20 minutes

10 minutes

4

Ingredients

- 17 ounces of minced meat
- 12 ounces of pasta
- 1 sweet red onion
- 2 garlic cloves
- 1 tablespoon of vegetable oil
- 3 tablespoons of tomato paste
- 2 ounces of grated Parmesan Cheese
- 3 bacon slices

Directions

1. Fry finely chopped onions and garlic in a frying pan in vegetable oil until it produces its characteristic smell.
2. Add minced meat and chopped bacon to the pan. Constantly break the lumps with a spatula and mix so that the minced meat is crumbly.
3. When the mince is ready, add tomato paste, mix, reduce heat, and leave to simmer.
4. At this time, boil the pasta.
5. When the pasta is ready, drain and arrange it on plates.
6. Add the meat sauce to the top of each serving of pasta. Serve topped with grated Parmesan.

Nutrition: Calories: 579; Fats: 21.7 g; Carbohydrates: 55.8 g; Protein: 37.4 g

Asparagus Pasta

10 minutes

25 minutes

6

Ingredients

- 8 ounces of farfalle pasta, uncooked
- 1 1/2 cup of asparagus, fresh, trimmed & chopped into 1-inch pieces
- 1 pint of grape tomatoes, halved
- 2 tablespoons of olive oil
- Sea salt & black pepper to taste
- 2 cups of mozzarella, fresh & drained
- 1/3 cup of basil leaves, fresh & torn
- 2 tablespoons of balsamic vinegar

Directions

1. Start by heating the oven to 400 degrees F.
2. Cook your pasta per package instructions, and reserve 1/4 cup of pasta water.
3. Get out a bowl and toss the tomatoes, oil, asparagus, and season with salt and pepper. Spread this mixture on a baking sheet, and bake for fifteen minutes. Stir twice.
4. Remove your vegetables from the oven, and then add the cooked pasta to your baking sheet. Mix with a few tablespoons of pasta water so that your sauce becomes smoother.
5. Mix in your basil and mozzarella, drizzling with balsamic vinegar. Serve warm.

Nutrition: Calories: 269; Protein: 10.8 g; Fats: 10.7 g; Carbohydrates: 32.5 g

Zucchini and Chicken

10 minutes

15 minutes

4

Ingredients

- 1 pound of chicken breasts, cut into medium chunks
- 12 ounces of zucchini, sliced
- 2 tablespoons of olive oil
- 2 garlic cloves, minced
- 2 tablespoons of parmesan, grated
- 1 tablespoon of parsley, chopped
- Salt and black pepper to taste

Directions

1. In a bowl, mix chicken pieces with 1 tablespoon oil, some salt, and pepper, and toss to coat.
2. Heat a pan over medium-high heat, add chicken pieces, brown for 6 minutes on all sides, transfer to a plate and leave aside.
3. Heat the pan with the remaining oil over medium heat, add zucchini slices and garlic, stir and cook for 5 minutes.
4. Return chicken pieces to the pan, add parmesan on top, stir, remove from the heat, divide between plates, and serve with some parsley on top.

Nutrition: Calories: 231; Fats: 10.8 g; Carbohydrates: 5.4 g; Protein: 28.7 g

Mediterranean Chili Beef

15 minutes

25 minutes

4

Ingredients

- 8 ounces of lean ground beef
- 4 minced garlic cloves
- 3/4 teaspoon of salt, divided
- 1/4 teaspoon of pepper
- 3 teaspoons of olive oil, divided
- 1 medium sliced red onion
- 2 medium zucchinis, sliced
- 1 medium-size green pepper
- 1 28 ounces can of diced tomatoes, undrained
- 1 teaspoon of red wine vinegar
- 1 teaspoon of dried basil
- 1 teaspoon of dried thyme

Directions

1. Sauté beef in 1/4 teaspoon salt, garlic, pepper, and a teaspoon of oil over medium heat until beef turns brown. Drain and remove. Keep warm.
2. Using the same skillet, pour the remaining oil and sauté the onion. Add zucchini and green pepper and stir-cook for 4 to 6 minutes until crisp-tender.
3. Stir in the remaining ingredients. Add beef and cook until heated through—serve with pasta or brown rice.

Nutrition: Calories: 197; Carbohydrates: 11.3 g; Fats: 10.9 g; Protein: 13.8 g

Chorizo-Kidney Beans Quinoa Pilaf

10 minutes

35 minutes

4

Ingredients

- 1/4 pound of dried Spanish chorizo diced (about 2/3 cup)
- 1/4 teaspoon of red pepper flakes
- 1/4 teaspoon of smoked paprika
- 1/2 teaspoon of cumin
- 1/2 teaspoon of sea salt
- 1 3/4 cups of water
- 1 cup of quinoa
- 1 large garlic clove minced
- 1 small red bell pepper finely diced
- 1 small red onion finely diced
- 1 tablespoon of tomato paste
- 1 15-ounce can of kidney beans rinsed and drained

Directions

1. Heat a non-stick pan on medium-high heat. Add chorizo and sauté for 5 minutes until lightly browned.
2. Stir in peppers and onion. Sauté for 5 minutes.
3. Add tomato paste, red pepper flakes, salt, paprika, cumin, and garlic. Sauté for 2 minutes.
4. Stir in quinoa and mix well. Sauté for 2 minutes.
5. Add water and beans. Mix well. Cover and simmer for 20 minutes or until liquid is fully absorbed.
6. Turn off the heat and fluff the quinoa. Let it sit for 5 minutes more while uncovered.
7. Serve and enjoy.

Nutrition: Calories: 277; Fats: 6.8 g; Carbohydrates: 47.8 g; Protein: 17.6 g

Halibut Fillets

10 minutes

20 minutes

4

Ingredients

- 4 halibut fillets, boneless
- 1 red bell pepper, chopped
- 2 tablespoons of olive oil
- 1 yellow onion, chopped
- 4 garlic cloves, minced
- 1/2 cup of chicken stock
- 1 teaspoon basil, dried
- 1/2 cup of cherry tomatoes, halved
- 1/3 cup of kalamata olives, pitted and halved
- Salt and black pepper to the taste

Directions

1. Heat a pan with the oil over medium heat, add the fish, cook for 5 minutes on each side, and divide between plates.
2. Add the onion, bell pepper, garlic, and tomatoes to the pan, stir and sauté for 3 minutes.
3. Add salt, pepper, and the rest of the ingredients, toss and cook for 3 minutes more. Place a portion next to each fillet and serve.

Nutrition: Calories: 210; Fats: 10.4 g; Carbohydrates: 7.5 g; Protein: 21.3 g

Vegetable and Red Lentil Stew

10 minutes

35 minutes

6

Ingredients

- 1 tablespoon extra-virgin olive oil
- 2 onions, peeled and finely diced
- 6 1/2 cups of water
- 2 zucchinis, finely diced
- 4 celery stalks, finely diced
- 3 cups of red lentils
- 1 teaspoon dried oregano
- 1 teaspoon salt, plus more as needed

Directions

1. Heat the olive oil in a large pot over medium heat.
2. Add the onions and sauté for about 5 minutes, stirring constantly, or until the onions are softened.
3. Stir in the water, zucchini, celery, lentils, oregano, and salt, and bring the mixture to a boil.
4. Reduce the heat to low and let simmer covered for 30 minutes, stirring occasionally, or until the lentils are tender.
5. Taste and adjust the seasoning as needed.
6. Tip: You can try this recipe with different lentils such as brown and green lentils, but they need additional cooking time, about 20 minutes.

Nutrition: Calories: 113; Fats: 2.1 g; Carbohydrates: 16.7 g; Protein: 6.9 g

Mashed Beans with Cumin & Egg Topper

10 minutes

10 to 12 minutes

4 to 6

Ingredients

- 1 tablespoon extra-virgin olive oil, plus extra for serving
- 4 garlic cloves, minced
- 1 teaspoon ground cumin
- 2 (15-ounce / 425-g) cans of fava beans
- 3 tablespoons of tahini
- 2 tablespoons of lemon juice, plus lemon wedges for serving
- Salt and pepper, to taste
- 1 tomato, cored and cut into 1/2-inch pieces
- 1 small onion, finely chopped
- 2 hard-boiled large eggs, chopped
- 2 tablespoons of finely chopped fresh parsley

Directions

1. Add the olive oil, garlic, and cumin to a medium saucepan over medium heat. Cook for about 2 minutes, or until fragrant.
2. Stir in the beans with their liquid and tahini. Bring to a simmer and cook for 8 to 10 minutes, or until the liquid thickens slightly.
3. Turn off the heat, and mash the beans to a coarse consistency with a potato masher. Stir in the lemon juice and 1 teaspoon of pepper. Season with salt and pepper.
4. Transfer the mashed beans to a serving dish. Top with the tomato, onion, eggs, and parsley. Drizzle with the extra olive oil.
5. Serve with lemon wedges.

Nutrition: Calories: 188; Fats: 4.6 g; Carbohydrates: 18.1 g; Protein: 18.4 g

Mediterranean Pasta with Tomato Sauce and Vegetables

15 minutes

25 minutes

4

Ingredients

- 8 ounces of linguine or spaghetti, cooked
- 1 teaspoon of garlic powder
- 1 (28 ounces) can of whole peeled tomatoes, drained and sliced
- 1 tablespoon of olive oil
- 1 (8 ounces) can of tomato sauce
- 1/2 teaspoon of Italian seasoning
- 8 ounces of mushrooms, sliced
- 8 ounces of yellow squash, sliced
- 8 ounces of zucchini, sliced
- 1/2 teaspoon of sugar
- 1/2 cup of grated Parmesan cheese

Directions

1. In a medium saucepan, mix tomato sauce, tomatoes, sugar, Italian seasoning, and garlic powder. Bring to the boil on medium heat. Reduce heat to low. Cover and simmer for 20 minutes.
2. In a large skillet, heat olive oil on a medium-high heat.
3. Add squash, mushrooms, and zucchini. Cook, stirring, for 4 minutes or until tender-crisp.
4. Stir vegetables into the tomato sauce.
5. Add pasta in a serving bowl.
6. Spoon the vegetable mixture over pasta and toss to coat.
7. Top with grated Parmesan cheese.

Nutrition: Calories: 398; Fats: 4.6 g; Carbohydrates: 70.6 g; Protein: 14.6 g

Baked Shrimp Mix

10 minutes

32 minutes

4

Ingredients

- 4 gold potatoes, peeled and sliced
- 2 fennel bulbs, trimmed and cut into wedges
- 2 shallots, chopped
- 2 garlic cloves, minced
- 3 tablespoons of olive oil
- 1/2 cup of kalamata olives, pitted and halved
- 2 pounds of shrimp, peeled and deveined
- 1 teaspoon lemon zest, grated
- 2 teaspoons of oregano, dried
- 4 ounces of feta cheese, crumbled
- 2 tablespoons of parsley, chopped

Directions

1. In a roasting pan, combine the potatoes with 2 tablespoons of oil, garlic, and the rest of the ingredients except the shrimp, toss, introduce to the oven and bake at 450 degrees F for 25 minutes.
2. Add the shrimp, toss, bake for 7 minutes more, divide between plates and serve.

Nutrition: Calories: 441; Fats: 21.3 g; Carbohydrates: 33.8 g; Protein: 28.8 g

---

Greek Turkey Burger

10 Minutes

10 Minutes

4

Ingredients

- 1 pound of ground turkey
- 1 medium zucchini, grated
- 1/4 cup of whole-wheat bread crumbs
- 1/4 cup of red onion, minced
- 1/4 cup of crumbled feta cheese
- 1 large egg, beaten
- 1 garlic clove, minced
- 1 tablespoon of fresh oregano, chopped
- 1 teaspoon of salt
- 1/4 teaspoon of freshly ground black pepper
- 1 tablespoon of extra-virgin olive oil

Directions

1. In a large bowl, combine the turkey, zucchini, bread crumbs, onion, feta cheese, egg, garlic, oregano, salt, and black pepper, and mix well. Shape into four equal patties.
2. Heat the olive oil in a large nonstick grill pan or skillet over medium-high heat.
3. Add the burgers to the pan and reduce the heat to medium.
4. Cook on one side for 5 minutes, then flip and cook on the other side for 5 minutes more.

Nutrition: Calories: 185; Fats: 6.5 g; Protein: 26.5 g; Carbohydrates: 4.9 g

Easy Fall-Off-the-Bone Ribs

15 minutes

8 hours

4

Ingredients

- 1 pound of baby back ribs
- 4 tablespoons of coconut amino
- 1/4 cup of dry red wine
- 1/2 teaspoon of cayenne pepper
- 1 garlic clove, crushed
- 1 teaspoon of Italian herb mix
- 1 tablespoon of butter
- 1 teaspoon of serrano pepper, finely chopped.
- 1 Italian pepper, thinly sliced
- 1 teaspoon of grated lemon zest

Directions

1. Grease the sides and bottom of the crockpot. Add the pork and peppers on the bottom.
2. Add in the remaining ingredients.
3. Slow cook for 9 hours on a low heat setting.

Nutrition: Calories: 223; Fats: 14.9 g; Carbohydrates: 4.5 g; Protein: 18.8 g

Marinated Tuna Steak

6 minutes

18 minutes

4

Ingredients

- 2 tablespoons of olive oil
- 1/4 cup of orange juice
- 1/4 cup of soy sauce
- 1 tablespoon of lemon juice
- 2 tablespoons of fresh parsley
- 1 garlic clove
- 1/2 teaspoon of ground black pepper
- 1/2 teaspoon of fresh oregano
- 4 tuna steaks (4 ounces steaks)

Directions

1. Mince the garlic and chop the oregano and parsley.
2. In a glass container, mix the pepper, oregano, garlic, parsley, lemon juice, soy sauce, olive oil, and orange juice.
3. Warm the grill using the high heat setting. Grease the grate with oil.
4. Add tuna steaks and cook for five to six minutes. Turn and baste with the marinated sauce.
5. Cook for another five minutes or until it's the way you like it. Discard the remaining marinade.

Nutrition: Calories: 209; Fats: 10.9 g; Carbohydrates: 2.5 g; Protein: 25.4 g

Garlic and Shrimp Pasta

4 minutes

16 minutes

4

Ingredients

- 6 ounces of whole-wheat spaghetti
- 12 ounces of raw shrimp, peeled and deveined, cut into 1-inch pieces
- 1 bunch of asparagus, trimmed
- 1 large bell pepper, thinly sliced
- 1 cup of fresh peas
- 3 garlic cloves, chopped
- 1 and 1/4 teaspoons of salt
- 1/2 and 1/2 cup of non-fat plain yogurt
- 3 tablespoons of lemon juice
- 1 tablespoon extra-virgin olive oil
- 1/2 teaspoon fresh ground black pepper
- 1/4 cup of pine nuts, toasted

Directions

1. Take a large-sized pot and bring water to a boil
2. Add your spaghetti and cook them for a few minutes less than the packet instructions.
3. Add shrimp, bell pepper, and asparagus and cook for about 2-4 minutes until the shrimp are tender.
4. Drain the pasta.
5. Take a large bowl and mash the garlic until a paste forms
6. Whisk in yogurt, parsley, oil, pepper, and lemon juice into the garlic paste
7. Add pasta, mix, and toss well
8. Serve by sprinkling some pine nuts!

Nutrition: Calories: 336; Fats: 11.5 g; Carbohydrates: 35.8 g; Protein: 23.1 g

Turkey and Asparagus Mix

10 minutes

30 minutes

4

Ingredients

- 1 bunch of asparagus, trimmed and halved
- 1 big turkey breast, skinless, boneless and cut into strips
- 1 teaspoon basil, dried
- 2 tablespoons of olive oil
- A pinch of salt and black pepper
- 1/2 cup of tomato sauce
- 1 tablespoon chives, chopped

Directions

1. Heat oil in a pan over a medium-high heat, add the turkey, and brown for 4 minutes.
2. Add the asparagus, and the rest of the ingredients except the chives, bring to a simmer and cook over medium heat for 25 minutes.
3. Add the chives, divide the mix between plates, and serve.

Nutrition: Calories: 172; Fats: 8.2 g; Carbohydrates: 2.8 g; Protein: 22.3 g

Easy Fish and Papillote Recipe

20 minutes

25 minutes

1-2

Ingredients

- 1 1/4 pounds of cod fillet (2.5 cm thick) cut into 4 pieces
- salt and black pepper
- 1/2 tomato thinly sliced into 4 rounds
- 1/2 cored green pepper, thinly sliced into 4 rounds
- 1/2 lemon cut into thin rings
- A handful of pitted green olives optional

FOR THE SAUCE:
- 1/4 cup of extra virgin olive oil
- Juice of 1/2 lemon
- 1 shallot finely chopped
- 2 garlic cloves finely chopped
- 1 teaspoon of oregano
- 1 teaspoon of paprika powder
- 1/2 teaspoon of cumin

Directions

1. Heat the oven to 425 degrees F.
2. Season the fish on both sides with salt and pepper.
3. Prepare the sauce. Add the olive oil, lemon juice, shallots, garlic, and herbs in a small mixing bowl or measuring cup and whisk to combine.
4. Prepare 4 large pieces of parchment paper (about 12 x 12 inches). Fold the parchment paper pieces lengthways in the middle to mark two halves.
5. Place each fish fillet on the bottom half of a piece of parchment paper and spoon 2 tablespoons of the prepared sauce over the fish. Add 1 slice of lemon, 1 slice of tomato, and 1 slice of bell pepper.
6. Fold the top half of the parchment paper over the fish and vegetables and fold and secure each piece of parchment around the fish and vegetables to create a well-packed pouch.
7. Place the fish bags on a large baking tray. Bake on the center rack of your heated oven for 12 to 15 minutes or until the fish is cooked through and falls apart easily.
8. To serve, place the fish and vegetables, in their closed parchment bags, on a serving platter.

Nutrition: Calories: 237; Fats: 17.1 g; Carbohydrates: 6.9 g; Protein: 16.7 g

Calamari with Tomato Sauce

20 minutes

8 minutes

4

Ingredients

- 3 pounds of calamari
- 1/3 cup of olive oil
- 1 tablespoon of fresh oregano
- 1 teaspoon of lemon juice
- 1 tablespoon of garlic, minced
- 1/4 teaspoon of chopped fresh lemon peel
- 1/4 teaspoon of crushed red pepper
- 1/4 cup of vinegar

SAUCE:
- 1 pound of fresh whole tomatoes
- 3 garlic cloves, minced
- 1 stalk of celery, chopped
- 1 tablespoon of olive oil
- 1/2 green bell pepper
- Salt and pepper to taste
- 1/2 cup of onion, chopped

Directions

1. To make the sauce, mix all the sauce ingredients and add them to the blender.
2. Blend until the mixture is smooth. Clean the calamari and slice it into 1/2-inch rings.
3. Season calamari with vinegar, red pepper, lemon peel, garlic, lemon juice, and oregano. Add oil to the air fryer. Add calamari with its juice. Air fry for about 6 minutes.
4. Stir once and air fry for another 2 minutes. Serve with hot sauce.

Nutrition: Calories: 307; Fats: 18.8 g; Carbohydrates: 3.2 g; Protein: 31.7 g

Kataifi-Wrapped Shrimp with Lemon-Garlic Butter

30 minutes

22 minutes

5

Ingredients

- 20 large green shrimps, peeled and deveined
- 7 tablespoons of unsalted butter
- 12 ounces of kataifi pastry
- Wedges of lemon or lime
- Salt and pepper to taste
- 5 garlic cloves, crushed
- 2 lemons, zested and juiced

Directions

1. In a pan, over low heat, melt the butter. Add the garlic and lemon zest, and sauté for about 2 minutes. Season with salt, pepper, and lemon juice.
2. Cover the shrimp with half of the garlic butter sauce and set aside the remaining half of the sauce.
3. Pre-heat your air fryer to 360 degrees F and cover the tray with a sheet of foil. Remove the pastry from its wrapping and tease out strands.
4. Lay 6-inch strands on a counter-top. Wrap each shrimp and some butter in the pastry. The shrimp tails should be exposed.
5. Repeat the process for all of the shrimp. Add the shrimp to the air fryer for 10 minutes.
6. Flip your shrimp over and add back into the air fryer for another 10 minutes.
7. Serve with a salad and lime or lemon wedges. Dip the shrimp into the remaining garlic butter sauce.

Nutrition: Calories: 304; Fats: 14.3 g; Carbohydrates: 30.5 g; Protein: 13.4 g

Salmon with Creamy Zucchini

15 minutes

10 minutes

2

Ingredients

- 2 (6-ounce) salmon fillets, skin on
- Salt and pepper to taste
- 1 teaspoon olive oil

COURGETTE:
- 2 large zucchinis, trimmed and spiralized
- 1 avocado, peeled and chopped
- A small handful of parsley, chopped
- 1/2 garlic clove, minced
- A small handful of cherry tomatoes, halved
- A small handful of black olives, chopped
- 2 tablespoons of pine nuts, toasted

Directions

1. Preheat your air fryer to 350 degrees F. Brush salmon with olive oil and season with salt and pepper.
2. Place the salmon in the air fryer and cook for 10 minutes.
3. Blend the avocado, garlic, and parsley in a food processor until smooth.
4. Toss in a bowl with zucchini, olives, and tomatoes.
5. Divide vegetables between two plates, top each portion with a salmon fillet, sprinkle with pine nuts, and serve.

Nutrition: Calories: 382; Fats: 21.3 g; Carbohydrates: 11.8 g; Protein: 36.7 g

Spicy Roasted Leg of Lamb

30 minutes

2 hours

4

Ingredients

FOR THE LAMB:
- 1 pound/450 g of a leg of lamb, bone-in
- Salt and pepper
- 3 tablespoons of olive oil
- 5 sliced garlic cloves
- 2 cups of water
- 4 cubed potatoes
- 1 onion, chopped
- 1 teaspoon of garlic powder

FOR THE LAMB SPICE RUB:
- 15 peeled garlic cloves
- 3 tablespoons of oregano
- 2 tablespoons of mint
- 1 tablespoon of paprika
- 1/2 cup of olive oil
- 1/4 cup of lemon juice

Directions

1. Allow the lamb to rest for 1 hour at room temperature.
2. While you wait, put all of the spice rub ingredients in a food processor and blend. Refrigerate the rub.
3. Make a few cuts in the lamb using a knife. Season with salt and pepper.
4. Place the lamb on a roasting pan.
5. Heat the broiler and broil for 5 minutes on each side so the whole thing is seared.
6. Place the lamb on the counter and set the oven temperature to 375 degrees F.
7. Let the lamb cool, then fill the cuts with the garlic slices and cover with the spice rub.
8. Pour 2 cups of water into the bottom of the roasting pan.
9. Sprinkle the potatoes and onions with garlic powder, salt, and pepper. Arrange them around the leg of lamb.
10. Add oil to the top of the lamb and vegetables.
11. Use aluminum foil to cover the roasting pan and return it to the oven.
12. Roast the lamb for 1 hour.
13. Discard the foil and roast for 15 minutes more.
14. Let the leg of lamb sit for 20 minutes before serving.

Nutrition: Calories: 413; Fats: 21 g; Carbohydrates: 31.2 g; Protein: 23.8 g

Dijon & Herb Pork Tenderloin

1hr

30 minutes

6

Ingredients

- 1/2 cup of freshly chopped Italian parsley leaves
- 3 tablespoons of fresh rosemary leaves, chopped
- 3 tablespoons of fresh thyme leaves, chopped
- 3 tablespoons of Dijon mustard
- 1 tablespoon of extra-virgin olive oil
- 4 garlic cloves, minced
- 1/2 teaspoon of sea salt
- 1/4 teaspoon of freshly ground black pepper
- 1 1/2 pound of pork tenderloin

Directions

1. Preheat the oven to 400 degrees F.
2. In a blender or food processor, combine the parsley, rosemary, thyme, mustard, olive oil, garlic, sea salt, and pepper. Process for about 30 seconds until smooth.
3. Spread the mixture evenly over the pork and add it on a rimmed baking sheet.
4. Bake for about 20 minutes, or until the meat reaches an internal temperature of 140 degrees F.
5. Allow to rest for 10 minutes before slicing and serving.

Nutrition: Calories: 223; Fats: 13.0 g; Carbohydrates: 1.9 g; Protein: 24.5 g

Grilled Lamb Gyro Burger

15 minutes

12 minutes

2

Ingredients

- 4 ounces/115 g of lean ground lamb
- 4 naan flatbread or pita
- 2 tablespoons of olive oil
- 2 tablespoons of tzatziki sauce
- 1 red onion, thinly sliced
- 1 tomato, sliced
- 1 bunch of lettuce, leaves separated

Directions

- Grill meat for 10 minutes.
- Toast naan bread, and drizzle with olive oil.
- Top two of the halves of naan bread with meat, and the rest of the ingredients.
- Cover with the other halves and enjoy!

Nutrition: Calories: 332; Fats: 6.5 g; Carbohydrates: 23.5 g; Protein: 15.2 g

A Great Mediterranean Snapper

11 minutes

19 minutes

2

Ingredients

- 2 tablespoons of extra virgin olive oil
- 1 medium onion, chopped
- 2 garlic cloves, minced
- 1 teaspoon oregano
- 1 can (14 ounces tomatoes), diced with juice
- 1/2 cup of black olives, sliced
- 4 red snapper fillets (each 4 ounces)
- Salt and pepper as needed
- Garnish
- 1/4 cup of feta cheese, crumbled
- 1/4 cup of parsley, minced

Directions

1. Pre-heat your oven to a temperature of 425 degrees F
2. Take a 13x9 inch baking dish and grease it with non-stick cooking spray
3. Take a large-sized skillet and put it on a medium heat
4. Add oil and heat it up
5. Add onion, oregano, and garlic
6. Sauté for 2 minutes
7. Add diced tomatoes with juice as well as the black olives
8. Bring the mix to a boil
9. Remove the heat
10. Add the fish on the prepped baking dish
11. Season both sides with salt and pepper
12. Spoon the tomato mix over the fish
13. Bake for 10 minutes
14. Remove the oven and sprinkle a bit of parsley and feta
15. Enjoy!

Nutrition: Calories: 440; Fats: 22.5 g; Carbohydrates: 12.5 g; Protein: 47 g

Pan-Fried Pork Chops with Orange Sauce

10 minutes

20 minutes

8

Ingredients

- 2 pounds/900 g of lean pork chops
- 3/4 teaspoon of salt
- 1/2 teaspoon of black pepper
- 2 tablespoons of olive oil
- 1 garlic clove
- 1/2 cup of orange juice
- 1 orange

Directions

1. Apply black pepper and salt to the pork chops.
2. In a medium heat pan, heat some olive oil and then fry the garlic.
3. Add the pork chops and sear them on both sides until tender and golden brown. Remove fried pork chops from the pan and set them aside.
4. Pour the orange juice into the same frying pan. Let it simmer for 4 minutes until the sauce thickens.
5. On a serving plate, add the pork chops with orange sauce and orange wedges.

Nutrition: Calories: 187; Fats: 10.7 g; Carbohydrates: 1.9 g; Protein: 22.5 g

Beef Spicy Salsa Braised Ribs

30 minutes

4 hours

12

Ingredients

- 6 pounds/2.7 kg of beef ribs
- 4 diced tomatoes
- 2 chopped jalapenos
- 2 chopped shallots
- 1 cup of chopped parsley
- 1/2 cup of chopped cilantro
- 3 tablespoons of olive oil
- 2 tablespoons of balsamic vinegar
- 1 teaspoon of worcestershire sauce
- Salt and pepper

Directions

1. Preheat the oven to 300 degrees F.
2. Combine all the ingredients in a baking dish except for the beef ribs.
3. Add the ribs and cover with aluminum foil.
4. Cook for 3 1/3 hours.
5. Serve the ribs warm.

Nutrition: Calories: 178; Fats: 11.6 g; Carbohydrates: 2.1 g; Protein: 17.2 g

Sage Turkey Mix

10 minutes

40 minutes

4

Ingredients

- 1 big turkey breast, skinless, boneless, and roughly cubed
- Juice of 1 lemon
- 2 tablespoons of avocado oil
- 1 red onion, chopped
- 2 tablespoons of sage, chopped
- 1 garlic clove, minced
- 1 cup of chicken stock

Directions

1. Heat the avocado oil in a pan over medium-high heat.
2. Add the turkey, and brown for 3 minutes on each side.
3. Add the remaining ingredients, bring to a simmer and cook over medium heat for 35 minutes.
4. Divide the mix between plates and serve with a side dish.

Nutrition: Calories: 159; Fats: 6.6 g; Carbohydrates: 2.6 g; Protein: 23.2 g

Grilled Seabass with Lemon Butter

10 minutes

40 minutes

2

Ingredients

- 1 pound of small potatoes
- 7 ounces of seabass fillets
- 1 teaspoon of olive oil
- 1/4 bunch of fresh thyme, chopped
- Green beans, cooked, optional

LEMON BUTTER SAUCE:
- 1 scallion, chopped
- 1/2 cup of thickened cream
- 1/2 cup of white wine
- 1 bay leaf
- 10 black peppercorns
- 1 garlic clove, chopped
- 8 ounces of unsalted butter
- 1 lemon, juiced
- Salt and pepper to taste

Directions

1. Preheat your air fryer to 390 degrees F for 5 minutes.
2. In a bowl, add potatoes, salt, thyme, and olive oil. Mix the ingredients well.
3. Put potatoes into the air fryer basket and cook for 20 minutes. Layer the fish fillets in a basket on top of the potatoes. Cook for another 20 minutes.
4. Prepare the sauce on top of the stove. Heat scallions and garlic over medium-high heat and add the peppercorns and bay leaf.
5. Pour in the wine and reduce the heat to low.
6. Add the thickened cream and stir to blend. Add the butter and whisk over low heat. When the butter has melted add salt, pepper, and lemon juice.
7. Strain the sauce to remove peppercorns and the bay leaf. Add the fish and potatoes on a serving plate, add sauce and serve with green beans.

Nutrition: Calories: 474; Fats: 20.6 g; Carbohydrates: 28.3 g; Protein: 22.8 g

Cod with Grapes, Pecans, Fennel & Kale

1 hour

15 minutes

2

Ingredients

- 2 fillets of cod (8-ounce)
- 3 cups of kale, minced
- 2 teaspoons of white balsamic vinegar
- 1/2 cup of pecans
- 1 cup of grapes, halved
- 1 small bulb of fennel, cut into inch-thick slices
- 4 tablespoons of extra-virgin olive oil
- Salt and black pepper to taste

Directions

1. Preheat your air fryer to 400 degrees F. Use salt and pepper to season your fish fillets. Drizzle with 1 teaspoon of olive oil.
2. Add the fish to the air fryer with the skin side down and cook for 10 minutes. Take the fish out and cover loosely with aluminum foil.
3. Combine fennel, pecans, and grapes. Pour 2 tablespoons of olive oil and season with salt and pepper. Add to the air fryer basket. Cook for an additional 5 minutes.
4. In a bowl, combine minced kale and cooked grapes, fennel, and pecans.
5. Cover ingredients with balsamic vinegar and the remaining tablespoon of olive oil. Toss gently. Serve fish with sauce and enjoy!

Nutrition: Calories: 452; Fats: 29.2 g; Carbohydrates: 10.6 g; Protein: 35.3 g

Pork Loin & Orzo

20 minutes

30 minutes

4

Ingredients

- 1 pound of pork tenderloin
- 1 teaspoon of coarsely ground pepper
- 1 teaspoon of salt
- 2 tablespoons of olive oil
- 1 cup of uncooked orzo pasta
- Water as needed
- 2 cups of spinach
- 1 cup of cherry tomatoes
- 3/4 cup of crumbled feta cheese

Directions

1. Coat the pork loin with salt and black pepper and massage it into the meat. Then cut the meat into one-inch cubes.
2. Heat the olive oil in a cast-iron skillet over medium heat until sizzling hot. Cook the pork for about 8 minutes until there's no pink left.
3. Cook the orzo in water according to the packet directions (adding a pinch of salt to the water).
4. Stir in the spinach and tomatoes and add the cooked pork.
5. Top with feta and serve.

Nutrition: Calories: 433; Fats: 18.3 g; Carbohydrates: 35.5 g; Protein: 31.8 g

Lamb Chops

10 minutes

20 minutes

4

Ingredients

- 4 ounces of trimmed lamb rib chops
- 4 tablespoons of olive oil
- 1 tablespoon of salt
- 1/2 teaspoon of black pepper
- 3 tablespoons of Balsamic vinegar
- Non-stick cooking spray

Directions

1. Mix one tablespoon of oil with the rind and juice in a Ziploc-type bag. Add the chops and coat well. Marinate at room temperature for ten minutes.
2. Remove it from the bag and season with pepper and salt.
3. Using the med-high heat setting; coat a pan with the spray. Add the lamb and cook for two minutes per side until it's the way you like it.
4. Pour the vinegar into a saucepan (med-high) and cook until it's syrupy or for about three minutes.
5. Drizzle the vinegar and the rest of the oil (1 teaspoon) over the lamb.
6. Serve with your favorite sides.

Nutrition: Calories: 154; Fats: 13.5 g; Carbohydrates: 0 g; Protein: 7.8 g

---

Roasted Lamb with Vegetables

20 minutes

1 hour

4

Ingredients

- 1 pound of lamb leg shanks
- 1/2 tablespoon of dried Italian seasoning
- 1/4 teaspoon of salt
- 1/4 teaspoon of black pepper
- 2 tablespoons of olive oil
- 1 garlic clove
- 1 onion
- 2 carrots
- 1 potato
- 2 apples
- 2 rosemary sprigs

Directions

1. Season the lamb shanks with Italian seasoning, salt, and fresh ground black pepper.
2. Preheat the oven to 370 degrees F.
3. Add lamb to the greased baking dish, cover with foil and bake for 40 minutes.
4. Meanwhile, in a pan on medium high heat, sauté the garlic and onion in olive oil.
5. Add the carrots and potatoes, and sauté for another 3-5 minutes.
6. Transfer vegetables to the baking dish around the lamb and add the apples.
7. Bake the lamb with vegetables for another 20 minutes without foil until golden brown outside and tender inside.
8. Garnish with fresh rosemary.

Nutrition: Calories: 241; Fats: 12.8 g; Carbohydrates: 7.6 g; Protein: 23.8 g

Herbed Almond Turkey

10 minutes

40 minutes

4

Ingredients

- 1 big turkey breast, skinless, boneless, and cubed
- 1 tablespoon olive oil
- 1/2 cup of chicken stock
- 1 tablespoon basil, chopped
- 1 tablespoon rosemary, chopped
- 1 tablespoon oregano, chopped
- 1 tablespoon parsley, chopped
- 3 garlic cloves, minced
- 1/2 cup of almonds, toasted and chopped
- 3 cups of tomatoes, chopped

Directions

1. Heat the oil in a pan over medium-high heat.
2. Add the turkey and the garlic, and brown for 5 minutes.
3. Add the stock and the rest of the ingredients, bring to a simmer over medium heat and cook for 35 minutes.
4. Divide the mix between plates, and serve.

Nutrition: Calories: 166; Fats: 7.2 g; Carbohydrates: 5.8 g; Protein: 19.6 g

Air-Fried Fish

20 minutes

20 minutes

2

Ingredients

- 1 medium sea bass or halibut (12-ounce)
- 2 garlic cloves, minced
- 1 tablespoon olive oil
- 3 slices of ginger, julienned
- 2 tablespoons of cooking wine
- 1 tomato, cut into quarters
- 1 lime, thinly cut
- 1 green onion, chopped
- 1 chili, diced

Directions

1. Prepare ginger, garlic, and oil mixture: sauté ginger and garlic with oil until golden brown in a small saucepan over medium heat on top of the stove. Preheat your air fryer to 360 degrees F.
2. Prepare fish: clean, rinse, and pat dry. Cut in half to fit into the air fryer. Place the fish inside of air fryer basket then drizzle it with cooking wine.
3. Layer tomato and lime slices on top of the fish. Cover with garlic ginger oil mixture.
4. Top with green onion and slices of chili. Cover with aluminum foil. Cook for 20 minutes.

Nutrition: Calories: 235; Fat: 9.2 g; Carbs: 9.5 g; Protein: 29.2 g

Seasoned Pork Chops

10 minutes

4 hours

4

Ingredients

- 4 pork chops
- 2 garlic cloves, minced
- 1 cup chicken broth
- 1 tablespoon poultry seasoning
- 1/4 cup olive oil
- Pepper and salt

Directions

1. In a bowl, whisk together olive oil, poultry seasoning, garlic, broth, pepper, and salt.
2. Pour olive oil mixture into the slow cooker then place pork chops.
3. Cover and cook on high for 4 hours.
4. Serve and enjoy.

Nutrition: Calories 327; Fat 25.8g; Carbohydrates 0.8 g; Protein 23.1 g

Halibut Roulade

5 minutes

10 minutes

6

Ingredients

- 1 pound of halibut fillet
- 1/2 pound of shrimp
- 3 limes
- 1/2 bunch of cilantro
- 3 garlic cloves
- 1/2 leek
- 1 tablespoon of olive oil
- Freshly-cracked black pepper
- 1 cup of seafood demi-glace reduction sauce

Directions

1. Before starting, soak 12 wooden skewers in water for a minimum of 2 hours. Preheat the grill.
2. For the fillet, wash and chill and remove the shell and tail of the shrimp. Slice the shrimp in half along the length and remove the vein.
3. Squeeze the juice from 2 limes and cut one lime into wedges. Grate the rind for zest.
4. Reserve a quarter of the cilantro, chopping what remains. Slice the leek and mince the garlic.
5. Cut the halibut fillet across the length to about 1/2-3/4 inch thick. Spread and layer with shrimp, zest, cilantro, leek, and garlic, then carefully roll the halibut up.
6. Cut the fillet into 6 pinwheels and insert 2 skewers into each pinwheel forming X. Brush with oil and grill for 4 minutes per side or until it is golden brown.
7. Drizzle with oil and garnish with the remaining cilantro, zest, and 1/2 teaspoon of pepper. Serve with demi-glace reduction sauce.

Nutrition: Calories: 192; Carbohydrates: 4.2 g; Protein: 25.6 g; Fats: 8.3 g

Paprika Butter Shrimps

6 minutes

31 minutes

2

Ingredients

- 1/4 tablespoon smoked paprika
- 1/8 cup of sour cream
- 1/2 pound of tiger shrimps
- 1/8 cup of butter
- Salt and black pepper, to taste

Directions

1. Pre-heat the oven to 390 degrees F and grease a baking dish.
2. Mix together all the ingredients in a large bowl and transfer them to the baking dish.
3. Put them in the oven and bake for about 15 minutes.
4. Divide the shrimp into 2 to serve.

Nutrition: Calories: 179; Fats: 10.5 g; Carbohydrates: 2.1 g; Protein: 18.2 g

Turkey with Basil & Tomatoes

10 minutes

20 minutes

4

Ingredients

- 4 turkey breast fillets
- 1 tablespoon olive oil
- 1/4 cup of fresh basil, chopped
- 1 1/2 cup of cherry tomatoes, sliced in half
- 1/4 cup of olive tapenade

Directions

1. Season the turkey fillets with salt.
2. Add the olive oil to a saute pan.
3. Cook the turkey until brown on both sides.
4. Stir in the basil, tomatoes, and olive tapenade.
5. Cook for 3 minutes, stirring frequently.

Nutrition: Calories: 185; Fats: 7.5 g; Carbohydrates: 3.8 g; Protein: 22.5 g

Honey Balsamic Chicken

20 minutes

1 Hour

10

Ingredients

- 1/4 cup of honey
- 1/2 cup of balsamic vinegar
- 1/4 cup of soy sauce
- 2 garlic cloves minced
- 10 chicken drumsticks

Directions

1. Mix the honey, vinegar, soy sauce, and garlic in a bowl.
2. Marinate the chicken in the sauce for 30 minutes.
3. Put into a pressure cooker and cook on high pressure for 10 minutes.
4. Release the pressure quickly. Your food is ready to serve

Nutrition: Calories: 98; Fats: 3.5 g; Carbohydrates: 4.8 g; Protein: 12.1 g

Easy Baked Vegetables & Sausages

5 minutes

1 hour and 15 minutes

6

Ingredients

- 2 pounds of brussels sprouts, trimmed
- 3 pounds of butternut squash, peeled, seeded, and cut into the same size as sprouts
- 1 pound of pork breakfast sausages.
- 1 tablespoon of fat from the fried sausages.

Directions

1. Grease a 9x13 inch baking pan and preheat the oven to 350 degrees F.
2. On medium-high heat, add a large nonstick saucepan and cook the sausages. Break up the sausages and cook until browned.
3. In a greased pan mix browned sausage, squash, sprouts, sea salt, and fat. Toss to mix well. Pop into the oven and cook for an hour.
4. Remove from the oven and serve warm.

Nutrition: Calories: 231; Fats: 11.8 g; Carbohydrates: 18.3 g; Protein: 15.1 g

Quinoa Chicken Fingers

10 minutes

10 minutes

6

Ingredients

- 2 pounds/900 g of sliced chicken breasts
- 2 egg whites
- 1 1/2 cup of quinoa, cooked
- 1/2 cup of breadcrumbs
- 2 tablespoons of olive oil
- Salt, black pepper, paprika

Directions

1. Season chicken with salt, pepper, and paprika.
2. Dip the chicken in the egg whites, then coat with quinoa and breadcrumbs.
3. Cook the chicken in oil for 5 minutes on each side.

Nutrition: Calories: 292; Fats: 6.7 g; Carbohydrates: 19.2 g; Protein: 38.8 g

Chicken Wild Rice Soup

10 minutes

15 minutes

6

Ingredients

- 2/3 cup of wild rice, uncooked
- 1 tablespoon of onion, finely chopped
- 1 tablespoon of fresh parsley, chopped
- 1 cup of carrots, chopped
- 8 ounces of chicken breast, cooked
- 2 tablespoons of butter
- 1/4 cup of all-purpose white flour
- 5 cups of low-sodium chicken broth
- 1 tablespoon of slivered almonds

Directions

1. Start by adding rice and 2 cups of broth along with 1/2 cup of water to a cooking pot. Cook the chicken until the rice is al dente and set it aside.
2. Add butter to a saucepan and allow it to melt.
3. Stir in the onion and sauté until soft then add the flour and the remaining broth.
4. Stir it and then cook for 1 minute then add the chicken, cooked rice, and carrots. Cook for 5 minutes on simmer. Garnish with almonds. Serve immediately.

Nutrition: Calories: 234; Fats: 6.2 g; Carbohydrates: 28.8 g; Protein: 6.2 g

Classic Chicken Soup

10 minutes

25 minutes

2

Ingredients

- 1 1/2 cup of low-sodium vegetable broth
- 1 cup of water
- 1/4 teaspoon poultry seasoning
- 1/4 teaspoon black pepper
- 1 cup of chicken strips
- 1/4 cup of carrot
- 2 ounces of egg noodles, uncooked

Directions

1. Put all the ingredients in a slow cooker and toss with a large spoon.
2. Cook on high heat for 25 minutes.
3. Serve warm.

Nutrition: Calories: 223; Fats: 8.2 g; Carbohydrates: 14.0 g; Protein: 23.8 g

Turkey Verde with Brown Rice

15 minutes

30 minutes

5

Ingredients

- 2/3 cup of chicken broth
- 1 1/4 cup of brown rice
- 1 1/2 pound of turkey tenderloins
- 1 onion, sliced
- 1/2 cup of salsa verde

Directions

1. Add the chicken broth and rice to a pressure cooker.
2. Top with the turkey, onion, and salsa.
3. Close the pot and cook at high pressure for 18 minutes.
4. Release the pressure naturally.
5. Wait for 8 minutes before opening the pot.

Nutrition: Calories: 262; Fats: 4.3 g; Carbohydrates: 23.6 g; Protein: 29.8 g

Lemon Garlic Chicken

30 minutes

1 hour and 20 minutes

6

Ingredients

- 6 chicken breast fillets
- 3 tablespoons of olive oil
- 1 tablespoon lemon juice
- 3 garlic cloves, crushed and minced
- 2 teaspoons of dried parsley

Directions

1. Marinate the chicken breast fillets in a mixture of olive oil, lemon juice, garlic, parsley, and a pinch of salt and pepper.
2. Allow it to sit for 1 hour covered in the refrigerator.
3. Heat up a saute pan with vegetable oil to medium heat.
4. Cook the chicken for 5-7 minutes, turning once, or until fully cooked.

Nutrition: Calories: 197; Fats: 8.8 g; Carbohydrates: 0.7 g; Protein: 28.5 g

Sweet Chickpea and Mushroom Stew

10 minutes

8 minutes

4

Ingredients

- 1/2 tablespoon button mushrooms, chopped
- 1 cup of chickpeas, cooked
- 2 carrots, chopped
- 2 garlic cloves, crushed
- 4 cherry tomatoes
- 1 onion, peeled and chopped
- A handful of string beans, trimmed
- 1 apple, cut into 1-inch cubes
- 1/2 cup of raisins
- A handful of fresh mint
- 1 teaspoon ginger, grated
- 1/2 cup of orange juice, squeezed
- 1/2 teaspoon salt

Directions

1. Add all ingredients to a pressure cooker
2. Pour water over to cover
3. Cook on high pressure for 8 minutes
4. Quick-release the pressure over 10 minutes
5. Serve and enjoy!

Nutrition: Calories: 116; Fats: 0.7 g; Carbohydrates: 20.5 g; Protein: 6.8 g

Spinach-Stuffed Sole

5 minutes

20 minutes

4

Ingredients

- 4 (6-oz) sole fillets
- 4 scallions with ends trimmed and sliced
- A 1-pound pack of frozen spinach (thawed)
- 1 teaspoon of salt
- 3 teaspoons of chopped fennel
- 1/2 teaspoon of pepper
- 1 teaspoon of sweet paprika
- 2 tablespoons of lemon

Directions

1. Preheat the oven to 400 degrees F
2. Put a small pan on medium heat, then add 2 tablespoons of oil and heat for 3 seconds.
3. Add the scallion and cook for 3-4 minutes; allow it to cool.
4. In a bowl, add the scallions, spinach, pepper, 1/2 teaspoon of salt, and 1/4 teaspoon of pepper. Mix the ingredients
5. Rinse and dry the fillet with a paper towel. Massage the fish with oil and sprinkle with pepper, paprika, and 2 tablespoons of lemon.
6. Spread the spinach filling on the fillets and roll up each fillet starting from the wide angle. Secure each fillet with toothpicks.
7. Bake for 15-20 minutes. Remove the toothpick and sprinkle with lemon zest. Serve immediately.

Nutrition: Calories: 196; Carbohydrates: 9.3 g; Fats: 3.5 g; Protein: 32.3 g

Grilled Sardines

5 minutes

15 minutes

4

Ingredients

- 2 pounds of fresh sardine (clean gutted and scaled with the head removed)
- 2 teaspoons of salt
- 3 tablespoons of vegetable oil
- 3/4 teaspoon of pepper
- 1 1/2 teaspoons of dried oregano
- 3 tablespoons of lemon juice
- 1/2 cup of extra-virgin olive oil (divided)

Directions

1. Preheat your grill to a medium-high temperature.
2. Rinse the sardine and pat dry with a paper towel. Next, rub both sides with olive oil and sprinkle with pepper and salt.
3. Wipe the grill surface with oil. Place each sardine on the grill and grill for 2-3 minutes; while grilling, drizzle the sardine with olive oil, and lemon juice.
4. Sprinkle with oregano and serve.

Nutrition: Calories: 261; Carbohydrates: 2.6 g; Protein: 2933 g; Fats: 14.6 g

Brie-Stuffed Meatballs

15 minutes

25 minutes

5

Ingredients

- 2 eggs, beaten
- 1 pound of ground pork
- 1/3 cup of double cream
- 1 tablespoon fresh parsley
- salt and ground black pepper
- 1 teaspoon dried rosemary
- 10 (1-inch cubes) of brie cheese
- 2 tablespoons of scallions, minced
- 2 garlic cloves, minced

Directions

1. Preheat the oven to 390 degrees F
2. Mix all ingredients, except for the brie, until everything is well combined.
3. Roll the mixture into 10 patties.
4. Add cheese in the center of each patty and roll each one into a ball.
5. Roast for about 20 minutes.

Nutrition: Calories: 280; Fats: 18.8 g; Carbohydrates: 1.3 g; Protein: 26.4 g

Mediterranean Chicken

10 minutes

20 minutes

6

Ingredients

- 2 pounds of chicken breast fillet, sliced into strips
- Wine mixture (1/4 cup of white wine mixed with 3 tablespoons of red wine)
- 2 tablespoons of light brown sugar
- 1 1/2 teaspoons of dried oregano
- 6 garlic cloves, chopped

Directions

1. Pour the wine mixture into a pressure cooker.
2. Stir in the rest of the ingredients.
3. Toss the chicken to coat evenly.
4. Seal the pot.
5. Set it to high pressure.
6. Cook for 10 minutes.
7. Release the pressure naturally.

Nutrition: Calories: 180; Fats: 4.3 g; Carbohydrates: 4.7 g; Protein: 31.5 g

Duck and Blackberries

10 minutes

25 minutes

4

Ingredients

- 4 duck breasts, boneless with the skin scored
- 2 tablespoons of balsamic vinegar
- Salt and black pepper to taste
- 1 cup of chicken stock
- 4 ounces of blackberries
- 1/4 cup of chicken stock
- 2 tablespoons of avocado oil

Directions

1. Preheat oven to 365 F. When heated, place the duck breasts in a greased pan and cook for 20 minutes
2. Meanwhile, simmer the blackberries in a small pan for about 5 minutes, adding gradually the avocado oil. Crush the berries, then set aside
3. Once most of the fat has been expelled from the duck, remove most of this fat and turn the duck over. Allow to cook about 2 more minutes
4. In the meantime, simmer the remaining ingredients and add the blackberry sauce
5. Slice the duck and serve with the sauce

Nutrition: Calories: 298; Fats: 15.8 g; Carbohydrates: 7.3 g; Protein: 32.3 g

Turkey and Cranberry Sauce

10 minutes

50 minutes

4

Ingredients

- 1 cup of chicken stock
- 2 tablespoons of avocado oil
- 1/2 cup of cranberry sauce
- 1 big turkey breast, skinless, boneless, and sliced
- 1 yellow onion, roughly chopped
- Salt and black pepper to taste

Directions

1. Pre-heat the oven at 350 degrees F
2. Heat a pan with the avocado oil over medium-high heat. Then, add the onion and sauté for 5 minutes.
3. Add the turkey and brown for 5 minutes more.
4. Add the rest of the ingredients, toss and cook in the oven for 40 minutes

Nutrition: Calories: 125; Fats: 11.6 g; Carbohydrates: 6.6 g; Protein: 24.5 g

Salmon with Dill Sauce

20 minutes

23 minutes

4

Ingredients

- 1 1/2 pound of salmon
- 4 teaspoons of olive oil
- Pinch of sea salt

Dill Sauce:

- 1/2 cup of non-fat Greek yogurt
- 1/2 cup of light sour cream
- 2 tablespoons of dill, finely chopped
- Pinch of sea salt

Directions

1. Preheat your air fryer to 270 degrees F. Cut salmon into four 6-ounce portions and drizzle 1 teaspoon of olive oil over each piece.
2. Season with sea salt. Add salmon to the cooking basket and cook for 23 minutes.
3. Make dill sauce: In a mixing bowl, mix sour cream, yogurt, chopped dill, and sea salt.
4. Top cooked salmon with sauce and garnish with additional dill and serve.

Nutrition: Calories: 380; Fats: 24.2 g; Carbohydrates: 1.8 g; Protein: 38.8 g

Grilled Salmon with Capers & Dill

30 minutes

8 minutes

2

Ingredients

- 1 teaspoon capers, chopped
- 2 sprigs of dill, chopped
- The zest of 1 lemon
- 1 tablespoon olive oil
- 4 slices of lemon (optional)
- 11-ounce salmon fillet

Dressing:

- 5 capers, chopped
- 1 sprig of dill, chopped
- 2 tablespoons of plain yogurt
- A pinch of lemon zest
- Salt and black pepper to taste

Directions

1. Preheat your air fryer to 400 degrees F.
2. Mix dill, capers, lemon zest, olive oil, and salt in a bowl. Cover the salmon with this mixture. Cook salmon for 8 minutes.
3. Combine the dressing ingredients in another bowl.
4. When salmon is cooked, place it on a serving plate and drizzle dressing on top. Add lemon slices on the side of the plate and serve.

Nutrition: Calories: 341; Fats: 18.9 g; Carbohydrates: 6.3 g; Protein: 36.2 g

Mediterranean Tortellini

30 minutes

12 minutes

6

Ingredients

- 500 g of tortellini
- 250 g of dried tomatoes
- 2 onions
- 3 tablespoons of olive oil
- 3 tablespoons of white wine vinegar
- 1 teaspoon of thyme
- Salt and pepper
- 200 g of rocket

Directions

1. Cook the tortellini, drain and set aside.
2. Chop the onions and sauté them in olive oil with thyme. Add the chopped sun-dried tomatoes and fry for about 2 minutes. Then add the tortellini and remove the pan from the heat.
3. Season to taste with salt, pepper, and white wine vinegar. Finally, add the tomatoes and rocket. Finished! Serve and enjoy.

Nutrition: Calories: 346; Fats: 12.9 g; Carbohydrates: 48.3 g; Protein: 8.3 g

Sunday Chicken with Cauliflower Salad

15 minutes

20 minutes

2

Ingredients

- 1 teaspoon hot paprika
- 2 tablespoons of fresh basil, snipped
- 1/2 cup of mayonnaise
- 1 teaspoon mustard
- 2 teaspoons of butter
- 2 chicken wings
- 1/2 cup of cheddar cheese, shredded
- Sea salt
- Ground black pepper
- 2 tablespoons of dry sherry
- 1 shallot, finely minced
- 1/2 head of cauliflower

Directions

1. Boil the cauliflower with salted water in a pot until it has softened; cut into small florets and add them to a salad bowl.
2. Melt the butter in a saucepan over medium-high heat.
3. Cook the chicken for about 8 minutes or until the skin is crisp and browned. Season with hot paprika salt, and black pepper.
4. Whisk the mayonnaise, mustard, dry sherry, and shallot, and dress your salad.
5. Top the salad with cheddar cheese and fresh basil. Serve with the chicken wings.

Nutrition: Calories: 418; Fats: 28 g; Carbohydrates: 15.7 g; Protein: 25.6 g

Authentic Turkey Kebabs

15 minutes

30 minutes

6

Ingredients

- 1 1/2 pound of turkey breast, cubed
- 3 Spanish peppers, sliced
- 2 zucchinis, cut into thick slices
- 1 onion, cut into wedges
- 2 tablespoons of olive oil, room temperature
- 1 tablespoon dry ranch seasoning

Directions

1. Thread the turkey pieces and vegetables onto bamboo skewers. Sprinkle the skewers with dry ranch seasoning and olive oil.
2. Grill your kebabs for about 10 minutes, turning them periodically to ensure even cooking.
3. Wrap your kebabs in foil before packing them into airtight containers; keep them in your refrigerator for up to 3 days.

Nutrition: Calories: 175; Fats: 7.3 g; Carbohydrates: 4.5 g; Protein: 22.8 g

Neufchatel Turkey Bacon Bites

5 minutes

0 minutes

8

Ingredients

- 4 ounces of turkey bacon, chopped
- 4 ounces of Neufchatel cheese
- 1 tablespoon of butter, cold
- 1 jalapeno or red pepper, deveined and minced
- 1 teaspoon of oregano
- 2 tablespoons of scallions, finely chopped

Directions

1. Mix all of the ingredients in a mixing bowl. Roll the mixture into 8 balls. Serve.

Nutrition: Calories: 75; Fats: 5.1 g; Carbohydrates: 1.1 g; Protein: 6.8 g

Pistachio-Crusted Halibut

15 minutes

20 minutes

4

Ingredients

- 4 (6-oz) halibut fillet with skin removed
- 1/2 cup of shelled unsalted pistachios (chopped)
- 4 teaspoons of fresh parsley (chopped)
- 1 cup of bread crumbs
- 1/4 cup of extra-virgin olive oil
- 2 teaspoons of grated orange zest
- 1 teaspoon of grated lime zest
- 1/2 teaspoon of pepper
- 4 teaspoons of Dijon mustard
- 1 1/2 of salt

Directions

1. Preheat the oven to 400 degrees F.
2. In the food processor, add pistachio, zest, bread crumbs, parsley, and oil. Pulse until the ingredients are well combined.
3. Rinse the fish and pat dry with a paper towel. Season the fillet with salt and pepper.
4. Brush the fish with mustard, and divide the pistachio mix evenly with some on top of the fish. Press down the mixture to allow the crust to adhere.
5. Lining the baking sheet with baking paper, arrange the crusted fish, and bake for 20 minutes or until the fillet is golden brown. Leave for 5 minutes to cool, then serve.

Nutrition: Calories: 357; Carbohydrates: 8.5 g; Protein: 35.3 g; Fats: 20.4 g

Chapter 3
Side Dishes

Sweet Potato 'Toast'

5 minutes

15 minutes

4

Ingredients

- 2 plum tomatoes, halved
- 6 tablespoons of extra-virgin olive oil.
- Salt and freshly ground black pepper, to taste
- 2 large sweet potatoes, sliced lengthwise
- 1 cup of fresh spinach
- 8 medium asparagus, trimmed
- 4 large cooked eggs or egg substitute (poached, scrambled, or fried)
- 1 cup of arugula
- 4 tablespoons of pesto
- 4 tablespoons of shredded Asiago cheese

Directions

1. Preheat the oven to 450 degrees F.
2. On a baking sheet, brush the plum tomato halves with 2 tablespoons of olive oil and season with salt and pepper. Roast the tomatoes in the oven for approximately 15 minutes, then remove from the oven and allow to rest.
3. Put the sweet potato slices on a separate baking sheet and brush about 2 tablespoons of oil on each side. Season with salt and pepper.
4. Bake the sweet potato slices for about 15 minutes, flipping once after 5 to 7 minutes, when just tender. Remove from the oven and set aside.
5. In a sauté pan or skillet, heat the remaining 2 tablespoons of olive oil over medium heat and sauté the fresh spinach until just wilted.
6. Remove from the pan and rest on a paper towel-lined dish. In the same pan, add the asparagus and sauté, turning throughout. Transfer to a paper towel-lined dish.
7. Add the slices of grilled sweet potato on serving plates, and divide the spinach and asparagus evenly among the slices.
8. Add a prepared egg on top of the spinach and asparagus. Top this with 1/4 cup of arugula.
9. Finish by drizzling with 1 tablespoon of pesto and sprinkle with 1 tablespoon of cheese. Serve with 1 roasted plum tomato.

Nutrition: Calories: 322; Fats: 22.4 g; Carbohydrates: 22.3 g; Protein: 9.5 g

Millet Pilaf

20 minutes

11 minutes

4-5

Ingredients

- 1 cup of millet
- 1 cup of apricot and shelled pistachios (roughly chopped)
- 1 lemon juice and zest
- 1 tablespoon of olive oil
- 1 cup of parsley (fresh)

Directions

1. Pour one and three-quarter cups of water into your pressure cooker. Place the millet and put the lid on the pressure cooker.
2. Adjust time for 10 minutes on high pressure. When the time has elapsed, release pressure naturally.
3. Remove the lid and add all other ingredients. Stir while adjusting the seasonings.
4. Serve and enjoy

Nutrition: Calories: 169; Fat: 6.7 g; Carbs: 22.3 g; Protein: 5.1 g

Coconut Flour Spinach Casserole

25 minutes

30 minutes

6

Ingredients

- 8 eggs
- 5 ounces of chopped fresh spinach
- 1 cup of grated Parmesan cheese
- 1 teaspoon of salt
- 3/4 cup of coconut flour
- 3/4 cup of unsweetened almond milk
- 6 ounces of chopped artichoke hearts
- 3 minced garlic cloves
- 1/2 teaspoon of black pepper
- 1 tablespoon of baking powder

Directions

1. Preheat your air fryer to a temperature of about 375 degrees F. Grease your air fryer pan with cooking spray. Whisk the eggs with the almond milk, the spinach, the artichoke hearts, and 1/2 cup of parmesan cheese.
2. Add the garlic, salt, and pepper. Add the coconut flour and baking powder and whisk until very well combined.
3. Spread the mixture in your air fryer pan and sprinkle the remaining quantity of cheese on top.
4. Add the baking pan to the air fryer, lock it and set the timer to about 30 minutes. When the timer beeps, turn off your Air Fryer.
5. Remove the baking pan from the air fryer and sprinkle with the chopped basil. Slice, serve and enjoy.

Nutrition: Calories: 161; Carbohydrates: 9.4 g; Protein: 12.3 g; Fats: 8.3 g

Zucchini Fritters

10 minutes

30 Minutes

6

Ingredients

- 2 zucchinis, peeled & grated
- 1 sweet onion, finely diced
- 2 garlic cloves, minced
- 1 cup of parsley, fresh & chopped
- 1/2 teaspoon sea salt, fine
- 1/2 teaspoon black pepper, ground
- 2 tablespoons of olive oil
- 4 eggs, large

Directions

1. Line a plate with kitchen paper before setting it aside.
2. In a large bowl, mix your onion, parsley, garlic, zucchini, pepper, and sea salt.
3. In a different bowl, beat your eggs before adding them to your zucchini mixture. Make sure to combine these ingredients well.
4. Place a large skillet on a medium heat. Heat your olive oil, and then scoop 1/4 cup at a time into the skillet to create your fritters. Cook for three minutes or until the bottoms set. Flip and cook for an additional three minutes. Transfer them to your plate so they can drain. Serve with pita bread or on their own.

Nutrition: Calories: 58; Protein: 4.2 g; Fats: 3.6 g; Carbohydrates: 2.2 g

Sautéed Collard Greens

5 Minutes

45 Minutes

6

Ingredients

- 1 pound of fresh collard greens, cut into 2-inch pieces
- 1 pinch of red pepper flakes
- 3 cups of chicken broth
- 1 teaspoon of pepper
- 1 teaspoon of salt
- 2 garlic cloves, minced
- 1 large onion, chopped
- 3 slices of bacon
- 1 tablespoon of olive oil

Directions

1. Heat oil in a skillet on a medium-high heat.
2. Sauté bacon until crisp. Remove from the pan and crumble once it has cooled. Set aside.
3. Using the same pan, sauté onion, and cook until tender. Add garlic until aromatic. Add the collard greens and cook until they start to wilt.
4. Pour in the chicken broth and season with pepper, salt, and red pepper flakes. Lower the heat to low, then simmer for 45 minutes.

Nutrition: Calories: 64.2; Carbohydrates: 4.5 g; Protein: 2.2 g; Fats: 4.2 g

Roasted Cauliflower and Tomatoes

5 minutes

25 minutes

4

Ingredients

- 4 cups of cauliflower, cut into 1-inch pieces
- 6 tablespoons of extra-virgin olive oil.
- 4 cups of cherry tomatoes
- 1/2 teaspoon freshly ground black pepper
- 1/2 cup of grated Parmesan cheese

Directions

1. Preheat the oven to 425 degrees F.
2. Add the cauliflower, 3 tablespoons of the olive oil, and 1/2 teaspoon of salt to a large bowl and toss to evenly coat. Arrange the cauliflower in an even layer on the baking sheet.
3. In another large bowl, add the tomatoes, remaining 3 tablespoons of olive oil, and 1/2 teaspoon of salt, and toss to coat evenly. Pour onto a different baking sheet.
4. Put the sheet of cauliflower and the sheet of tomatoes in the oven to roast for 17 to 20 minutes until the cauliflower is lightly browned and the tomatoes are plump.
5. Using a spatula, spoon the cauliflower into a serving dish, and top with tomatoes, black pepper, and Parmesan cheese. Serve warm.

Nutrition: Calories: 234; Fats: 18.8 g; Carbohydrates: 10.3 g; Protein: 6.5 g

Butter Potatoes

10 minutes

30 minutes

6

Ingredients

- 1 1/2 pound of finger potatoes
- 1 tablespoon of dried rosemary
- 3 tablespoons of butter, softened
- 1 teaspoon salt

Directions

1. Pre-heat the oven to 375 degrees F.
2. Wash the finger potatoes well.
3. With the help of the big knife crush every potato.
4. Add the crushed potatoes to a baking tray and sprinkle with salt and dried rosemary. Mix well.
5. Bake the finger potatoes for 30 minutes. The cooked potatoes will be soft and have a light crust.

Nutrition: Calories: 134; Fats: 4.2 g; Carbohydrates: 21.7 g; Protein: 22.5 g

Mozzarella Eggplants

20 minutes

40 minutes

4

Ingredients

- 2 large eggplants
- 3 tomatoes
- 4 mozzarella balls
- 1 tablespoon olive oil
- 1 teaspoon salt

Directions

1. Trim the eggplants and make cross cuts to form 'hasselback' eggplants.
2. Sprinkle the vegetables with salt.
3. After this, slice the tomatoes and mozzarella balls.
4. Fill the eggplant cuts with Mozzarella and tomatoes, and sprinkle with olive oil.
5. Then wrap every eggplant in foil.
6. Bake the vegetables for 40 minutes at 375 degrees F.
7. Discard the foil from the eggplants and cut them into 4 servings (1/2 part of eggplant = 1 serving).

Nutrition: Calories: 310; Fats: 21.5 g; Carbohydrates: 10.7 g; Protein: 18.5 g

Sweet Potato Puree

10 minutes

15 minutes

6

Ingredients

- 2 pounds of sweet potatoes, peeled
- 1 1/2 cup of water
- 5 Medjool dates, pitted and chopped

Directions

1. Add all ingredients to a pot.
2. Close the lid and allow them to boil for 15 minutes until the potatoes are soft.
3. Drain the potatoes and put them in a food processor together with the dates.
4. Pulse until smooth.
5. Divide the mixture between individual containers.
6. Label and store containers in the fridge.
7. Allow them to thaw at room temperature before heating in the microwave.

Nutrition: Calories: 173; Fats: 0.3 g; Carbohydrates: 39.2 g; Protein: 3.3 g

Grilled Eggplant Rolls

30 minutes

10 minutes

5

Ingredients

- 2 large eggplants
- 4 ounces of goat cheese
- 1 cup of ricotta
- 1/4 cup of fresh basil, finely chopped

Directions

1. Slice off the tops of the eggplants and cut them lengthwise into 1/4-inch-thick slices. Sprinkle the slices with salt and add the eggplants to a colander for 15 to 20 minutes.
2. In a large bowl, combine the goat cheese, ricotta, basil, and pepper.
3. Preheat a grill, grill pan, or lightly oiled skillet on medium heat. Pat the eggplant slices dry using a paper towel and lightly spray with olive oil spray. Add the eggplant to the grill, grill pan, or skillet, and cook for 3 minutes on each side.
4. Take out the eggplant from the heat and allow it to cool for 5 minutes.
5. To roll, lay one eggplant slice flat, add a tablespoon of the cheese mixture at the base of the slice, and roll up. Serve immediately or chill until time to serve.

Nutrition: Calories: 129; Fats: 8.6 g; Carbohydrates: 4.9 g; Protein: 9.1 g

Vegetable-Stuffed Grape Leaves

50 minutes

45 minutes

7

Ingredients

- 2 cups of white rice, rinsed
- 2 large tomatoes, finely diced
- 1 (16-ounce) jar of grape leaves
- 1 cup of lemon juice
- 4 to 6 cups of water

Directions

1. In a bowl, mix the rice, tomatoes, 1 onion, 1 green onion, 1 cup of parsley, 3 garlic cloves, salt, and black pepper.
2. Drain and rinse the grape leaves.
3. Prepare a large pot by placing a layer of grape leaves on the bottom. Lay each leaf flat and trim off any stems.
4. Add 2 tablespoons of the rice mixture at the base of each leaf. Fold over the sides, then roll as tightly as possible. Place the rolled grape leaves in the pot, lining them up. Continue to layer in the rolled grape leaves.
5. Gently pour the lemon juice and olive oil over the grape leaves, and add enough water to just cover the grape leaves by 1 inch.
6. Lay a heavy plate that is smaller than the opening of the pot upside down over the grape leaves.
7. Cover the pot and cook the leaves over medium-low heat for 45 minutes. Allow them to stand for 20 minutes before serving.
8. Serve warm or cold.

Nutrition: Calories: 171; Fats: 0.3 g; Carbohydrates: 38.6 g; Protein: 4.3 g

Rustic Cauliflower and Carrot Hash

10 minutes

10 minutes

4

Ingredients

- 1 large onion, chopped
- 1 tablespoon of garlic, minced
- 2 cups of carrots, diced
- 4 cups of cauliflower pieces, washed
- 1/2 teaspoon of ground cumin

Directions

1. In a big skillet over medium heat, cook 3 tablespoons of olive oil, onion, garlic, and carrots for 3 minutes.
2. Cut the cauliflower into 1-inch or bite-size pieces. Add the cauliflower, salt, and cumin to the skillet and toss to combine with the carrots and onions.
3. Cover and cook for 3 minutes.
4. Toss the vegetables and continue to cook uncovered for an additional 3 to 4 minutes.
5. Serve warm.

Nutrition: Calories: 65; Fats: 12.5 g; Carbohydrates: 0.5 g; Protein: 2.5 g

Leek and Garlic Cannellini Beans

15 minutes

22 minutes

4

Ingredients

- 1 pound of dried cannellini beans, soaked overnight
- 1 onion, peeled and chopped
- 2 large leeks, finely chopped
- 3 garlic cloves, whole
- 1 teaspoon pepper
- 1 teaspoon salt
- 4 tablespoons of vegetable oil, for the topping
- 2 tablespoons of flour, for the topping
- 1 tablespoon cayenne pepper, for the topping

Directions

1. Add all the ingredients, except for the topping ingredients, to your pressure cooker.
2. Cook for 20 minutes on High
3. Take a skillet and heat 4 tablespoons of oil
4. Then add cayenne pepper and flour
5. Stir-fry for 2 minutes and keep them to one side
6. Once done, quickly release the pressure
7. Pour the cayenne mixture into the pot and give it a good stir
8. Let it sit for 15 minutes before you serve
9. Serve and enjoy!

Nutrition: Calories: 128; Fats: 11.3 g; Carbohydrates: 32.0 g; Protein: 14.3 g

Sweet Chickpea and Mushroom Stew

10 minutes

8 minutes

4

Ingredients

- 1/2 tablespoon button mushrooms, chopped
- 1 cup of chickpeas, cooked
- 2 carrots, chopped
- 2 garlic cloves, crushed
- 4 cherry tomatoes
- 1 onion, peeled and chopped
- A handful of string beans, trimmed
- 1 apple, cut into 1-inch cubes
- 1/2 cup of raisins
- A handful of fresh mint
- 1 teaspoon ginger, grated
- 1/2 cup of orange juice, squeezed
- 1/2 teaspoon salt

Directions

1. Add all ingredients to your pressure cooker
2. Pour water over to cover
3. Cook on high pressure for 8 minutes
4. Release the pressure naturally over a few minutes
5. Serve and enjoy!

Nutrition: Calories: 116; Fats: 0.7 g; Carbohydrates: 20.5 g; Protein: 6.8 g

Triumph of Cucumbers and Avocados

10 minutes

15 minutes

4

Ingredients

- 12 oz cherry tomatoes, cut in half
- 5 small cucumbers, chopped
- 3 small avocados, chopped
- 1/2 teaspoon of ground black pepper
- 2 tablespoons of olive oil
- 2 tablespoons of fresh lemon juice
- 1/4 cup of fresh cilantro, chopped
- 1 teaspoon of sea salt

Directions

1. Add cherry tomatoes, cucumbers, avocados, and cilantro to a large mixing bowl and mix well.
2. Mix together olive oil, lemon juice, black pepper, and salt and pour over salad.
3. Toss well and serve immediately.

Nutrition: Calories: 186; Fats: 2.2 g; Carbohydrates: 8.1 g; Protein: 2.2 g

Cheesy Spinach Pies

20 minutes

40 minutes

5

Ingredients

- 2 tablespoons of extra-virgin olive oil
- 3 (1-pound) bags of baby spinach, washed
- 1 cup of feta cheese
- 1 large egg, beaten
- Puff pastry sheets

Directions

1. Preheat the oven to 375 degrees F.
2. Using a big skillet over medium heat, cook the olive oil, 1 onion, and 2 garlic cloves for 3 minutes.
3. Add the spinach to the skillet one bag at a time, letting it wilt in between each bag. Toss using tongs. Cook for 4 minutes.
4. Once cooked, strain any extra liquid from the pan.
5. Mix the feta cheese, egg, and cooked spinach.
6. Lay the puff pastry flat on a counter. Cut the pastry into 3-inch squares.
7. Add a tablespoon of the spinach mixture in the center of a puff-pastry square. Turn over one corner of the square to the diagonal corner, forming a triangle. Crimp the edges of the pie together by pressing down with the prongs of a fork to seal them. Repeat until all squares are filled.
8. Place the pies on a parchment-lined baking sheet and bake for 25 to 30 minutes or until golden brown. Serve warm or at room temperature.

Nutrition: Calories: 176; Fats: 10.4 g; Carbohydrates: 11.4 g; Protein: 9.6 g

Greek-Style Beans

10 minutes

10 Hours And 40 minutes

8

Ingredients

- 3 cups of white beans
- 1/4 cup of olive oil
- 1 onion, diced
- 1 garlic clove, peeled
- 28 ounces of canned crushed tomatoes

Directions

1. Pour 8 cups of water into a pressure cooker. Add the white beans.
2. Season with a pinch of salt.
3. Let the beans soak for up to 10 hours.
4. Seal the pot and cook for 15 minutes at high pressure.
5. Release the pressure naturally.
6. Transfer the white beans into a bowl and set them aside.
7. Take 1 cup of the cooking liquid and set it aside.
8. Drain the remaining liquid.
9. Heat a saute pan with a little olive oil.
10. Cook the onion, garlic, and tomatoes for 5 minutes.
11. Add the reserved cooking liquid and the tomatoes.
12. Add all ingredients back into the pressure cooker.
13. Cook for 5 minutes at high pressure.
14. Release the pressure naturally.
15. Season with salt and pepper.

Nutrition: Calories: 193; Fats: 3.3 g; Carbohydrates: 29.4 g; Protein: 11.5 g

Simple Baked Okra

20 minutes

10 minutes

2

Ingredients

- 8 oz okra, chopped
- 1/2 teaspoon ground black pepper
- 1/2 teaspoon salt
- 1 tablespoon olive oil

Directions

1. Preheat the oven to 375 degrees F
2. Line the baking tray with foil.
3. Add the okra in the tray in one layer.
4. Sprinkle the vegetables with ground black pepper and salt. Mix well.
5. Next, drizzle the okra with olive oil.
6. Roast the vegetables for 10 minutes.
7. Stir the okra with the help of a spatula every 3 minutes.

Nutrition: Calories: 95; Fats: 5.2 g; Carbohydrates: 11.2 g; Protein: 1.3 g

Roasted Acorn Squash

10 minutes

35 minutes

6

Ingredients

- 2 acorn squash, medium to large
- 2 tablespoons of extra-virgin olive oil
- 5 tablespoons of unsalted butter
- 1/4 cup of chopped sage leaves
- 2 tablespoons of fresh thyme leaves

Directions

1. Preheat the oven to 400 degrees F.
2. Cut the acorn squash in half lengthwise. Scoop out the seeds and cut them horizontally into 3/4-inch-thick slices.
3. In a large bowl, drizzle the squash with the olive oil, sprinkle with salt, and toss together to coat.
4. Lay the acorn squash flat on a baking sheet.
5. Place the baking sheet in the oven and bake the squash for 20 minutes. Flip squash over with a spatula and bake for another 15 minutes.
6. Cook the butter in a medium saucepan over medium heat.
7. Sprinkle the sage and thyme in the melted butter and let them cook for 30 seconds.
8. Transfer the cooked squash slices to a plate. Spoon the butter/herb mixture over the squash. Season with salt and black pepper. Serve warm.

Nutrition: Calories: 144; Fats: 10.0 g; Carbohydrates: 11.2 g; Protein: 2.3 g

---

Sautéed Garlic Spinach

5 minutes

10 minutes

4

Ingredients

- 1/4 cup of extra-virgin olive oil
- 1 large onion, thinly sliced
- 3 garlic cloves, minced
- 6 bags of baby spinach, washed
- 1 lemon, cut into wedges

Directions

1. Cook the olive oil, onion, and garlic in a large skillet for 2 minutes over medium heat.
2. Add one bag of spinach and 1/2 teaspoon of salt. Cover the skillet and let the spinach wilt for 30 seconds. Repeat (omitting the salt), adding 1 bag of spinach at a time.
3. When all is added, open and cook for 3 minutes, letting some of the moisture evaporate.
4. Serve warm with lemon juice over the top.

Nutrition: Calories: 106; Fats: 6.3 g; Carbohydrates: 8.8 g; Protein: 3.8 g

Stuffed Sweet Potatoes

10 minutes

22 minutes

2

Ingredients

- 2 sweet potatoes (washed thoroughly)
- 1 cup of chickpeas
- 2 spring onions
- 1 avocado
- 1 cup of cooked couscous

Directions

1. Pour a cup and half of water into your i pressure cooker then place the steam rack in place.
2. Place the sweet potatoes on the rack. Set the valve to sealing and time for seventeen minutes under high pressure.
3. Meanwhile, roast the chickpeas in your pan with olive oil.
4. Add salt and pepper to taste then paprika. Stir until chickpeas are coated evenly.
5. Cook for a minute then put off the heat.
6. When the pressure cooker time elapses, release pressure naturally for five minutes. Let the sweet potatoes cool then remove them from the instant pot.
7. Cut the sweet potatoes lengthwise and use a fork to mash the inside creating a space for toppings.
8. Add the prepared toppings then serve with feta cheese lemon wedges.

Nutrition: Calories: 425; Fat: 11.2 g; Carbs: 67.5 g; Protein: 14.1 g

Garlicky Sautéed Zucchini with Mint

5 minutes

10 minutes

4

Ingredients

- 3 large green zucchinis
- 3 tablespoons of extra-virgin olive oil
- 1 large onion, chopped
- 3 garlic cloves, minced
- 1 teaspoon dried mint

Directions

1. Cut the zucchini into 1/2-inch cubes.
2. Put a large skillet over medium heat, and cook the olive oil, onions, and garlic for 3 minutes, stirring constantly.
3. Add the zucchini and salt to the skillet and toss to combine with the onions and garlic, cooking for 5 minutes.
4. Add the mint to the skillet, tossing to combine. Cook for another 2 minutes. Serve warm.

Nutrition: Calories: 91; Fats: 7.5 g; Carbohydrates: 5.6 g; Protein: 0.4 g

Mediterranean Parsnips and Peppers

15 minutes

1 hour

2

Ingredients

- 2 parsnips
- 1 bell pepper
- 1 garlic clove
- 50 g dried tomatoes
- 1 tablespoon balsamic vinegar
- Basil and chili flakes
- Salt and pepper
- Olive oil

Directions

1. Peel the parsnips and cut them into thin slices and cook in a saucepan with a little water for about 5 minutes.
2. Clean, core, and dice the peppers.
3. Heat olive oil in a pan and fry the chopped peppers and parsnip slices.
4. Peel and chop the garlic and add to the vegetables in the pan.
5. Season to taste with chili flakes, basil, pepper, and salt.
6. As soon as the pepper cubes and the parsnip slices are golden brown, put all the ingredients in a bowl and mix with the balsamic vinegar.
7. Finished! Serve and enjoy.

Nutrition: Calories: 103; Fats: 5.1 g; Carbohydrates: 12.1 g; Protein: 2.1 g

Stir fry Broccoli

5 Minutes

10 Minutes

6

Ingredients

- 3 tablespoons of olive oil
- 3 garlic cloves, minced
- 2 tablespoons of ginger, sliced
- 2 heads of broccoli, cut into florets
- Salt and pepper, to taste

Directions

1. Heat olive oil in a pot.
2. Sauté the garlic and ginger until fragrant, around 3 minutes.
3. Add the rest of the ingredients.
4. Stir fry until tender, around 7 minutes.

Nutrition: Calories: 99; Carbs: 2.8 g; Protein: 1.2 g; Fat: 9.6 g

Stewed Okra

5 minutes

25 minutes

4

Ingredients

- 4 garlic cloves, finely chopped
- 1 pound of fresh or frozen okra, cleaned
- 1 (15-ounce) can of plain tomato sauce
- 2 cups of water
- 1/2 cup of fresh cilantro, finely chopped

Directions

1. In a big pot at medium heat, stir and cook 1/4 cup of olive oil, 1 onion, garlic, and salt for 1 minute.
2. Stir in the okra and cook for 3 minutes.
3. Add the tomato sauce, water, cilantro, and black pepper; stir, cover, and let it cook for 15 minutes, stirring occasionally.
4. Serve warm.

Nutrition: Calories: 86; Fats: 1.3 g; Carbohydrates: 15.8 g; Protein: 3.4 g

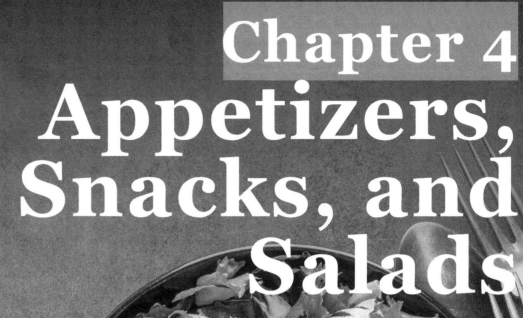

Chapter 4
Appetizers, Snacks, and Salads

Spicy Nuts

10 minutes

4 minutes

8

Ingredients

- 2 cups of mixed nuts
- 1 teaspoon of chipotle chili powder
- 1 teaspoon of salt
- 1 teaspoon of pepper
- 1 tablespoon of butter, melted
- 1 teaspoon of ground cumin

Directions

1. In a bowl, add all ingredients and toss to coat.
2. Preheat your air fryer to 350 degrees F for 5 minutes.
3. Add mixed nuts to the air fryer basket and roast for 4 minutes.

Nutrition: Calories: 88; Fats: 8.5 g; Carbohydrates: 0.2 g; Protein: 2.9 g

Easy Garbanzo Hummus

5 minutes

5 minutes

6

Ingredients

- 3 garlic cloves, crushed
- 1 tablespoon of olive oil
- 1 teaspoon of sea salt, fine
- 16 ounces of canned garbanzo beans, drained
- 1 1/2 tablespoon of tahini
- 1/2 cup of lemon juice, fresh

Directions

1. Blend your garbanzo beans, tahini, garlic, olive oil, lemon juice, and sea salt together for three to five minutes in a blender. Make sure it's mixed well. It should be fluffy and soft.
2. Refrigerate for at least an hour before serving with either pita bread or chopped vegetables.

Nutrition: Calories: 124.22; Protein: 10.8 g; Fats: 2.7 g; Carbohydrates: 15.5 g

Flatbread with Chicken Liver Pâté

15 minutes

2 hours 15 minutes

4

Ingredients

- 1 yellow onion, finely chopped
- 10 ounces of chicken livers
- 1/2 teaspoon Mediterranean seasoning blend
- 4 tablespoons of olive oil
- 1 garlic clove, minced

FOR FLATBREAD:
- 1 cup of lukewarm water
- 1/2 stick butter
- 1/2 cup of flax meal
- 1 1/2 tablespoon of psyllium husks
- 1 1/4 cups of almond flour

Directions

1. Pulse the chicken livers along with the seasoning blend, olive oil, onion, and garlic in your food processor; reserve.
2. Mix the dry ingredients for the flatbread. Mix in all the wet ingredients. Whisk to combine well.
3. Set aside at room temperature for 2 hours. Split the dough into 8 balls and roll them out on a flat surface.
4. In a lightly greased pan, cook your flatbread for 1 minute on each side or until golden.

Nutrition: Calories: 340; Fats: 24.8 g; Carbohydrates: 17.6 g; Protein: 12.9 g

Mediterranean Chickpea Salad

15 minutes

10 minutes

4

Ingredients

- 265 g of chickpeas
- 200 g of feta cheese
- 1 onion
- 1 bell pepper
- 1/2 cucumber
- 2 tablespoons of olives
- 2 tablespoons of parsley
- Salt and pepper

FOR THE DRESSING:
- 50 ml of olive oil
- 50 ml of white wine vinegar
- 1 tablespoon of lime juice
- 1 teaspoon of chili flakes
- Salt and pepper

Directions

1. Drain the chickpeas, wash and add them to a large bowl.
2. Cut the cucumber into slices. Core and chop the olives. Dice the paprika and feta, chop the onion, and chop the parsley.
3. Combine all ingredients, except for the dressing, in a bowl.
4. For the dressing: mix olive oil, white wine vinegar, lime juice, chili flakes, salt, and pepper well.
5. Add the dressing to the other ingredients and mix everything well. Finished! Serve and enjoy.

Nutrition: Calories: 205; Fats: 6.3 g; Carbohydrates: 14.8 g; Protein: 17.8 g

Celeriac Cauliflower Dip 113

10 minutes

12 minutes

6

Ingredients

- 1 head cauliflower
- 1 small celery root
- 1/4 cup of butter
- 1 tablespoon of chopped rosemary
- 1 tablespoon of chopped thyme
- 1 cup of cream cheese

Directions

1. Peel the celery root and cut it into small pieces.
2. Cut the cauliflower into similar-sized pieces and combine.
3. Toast the herbs in the butter in a large pan, until they become fragrant.
4. Add the cauliflower and celery root and stir to combine.
5. Season and cook on medium-high until all moisture has been released by the vegetables.
6. Cover and cook on low for 10-12 minutes.
7. Once the vegetables are soft, remove from the heat and add to a blender.
8. Make it smooth, then add the cream cheese and puree again.
9. Season and serve.

Nutrition: Calories: 73; Fats: 6.2 g; Carbohydrates: 2.2 g; Protein: 2.6 g

Fondue with Tomato Sauce 114

10 minutes

30 minutes

4

Ingredients

- 1 garlic clove, halved
- 6 medium tomatoes, seeded and diced
- 2/3 cup of dry white wine
- 6 tablespoons of butter, cubed
- 1-1/2 teaspoons of dried basil
- Dash cayenne pepper
- 2 cups of grated cheddar or similar cheese
- 1 tablespoon of all-purpose flour
- 1 cubed French bread stick.

Directions

1. Rub the bottom and sides of a fondue pot with a garlic clove.
2. Set aside and discard the garlic.
3. Combine wine, butter, basil, cayenne, and tomatoes in a large saucepan.
4. On medium-low heat, bring the mixture to a simmer, then decrease the heat to low.
5. Mix cheese with flour.
6. Add this to the tomato mixture gradually while stirring after each addition until the cheese is melted.
7. Pour into the preparation fondue pot and keep warm.
8. Enjoy with shrimp and bread cubes.

Nutrition: Calories: 169; Fats: 14.1 g; Carbohydrates: 5.8 g; Protein: 5.2 g

Bean and Toasted Pita Salad

15 minutes

10 minutes

4

Ingredients

- 3 tablespoons of chopped fresh mint
- 3 tablespoons of chopped fresh parsley
- 1 cup of crumbled feta cheese
- 1 cup of sliced romaine lettuce
- 1/2 cucumber, peeled and sliced
- 1 cup of diced plum tomatoes
- 2 cups of cooked pinto beans, well-drained and slightly warmed
- Pepper to taste
- 3 tablespoons of extra virgin olive oil
- 2 tablespoons of ground toasted cumin seeds
- 2 tablespoons of fresh lemon juice
- 1/8 teaspoons of salt
- 2 garlic cloves, peeled
- 2 6-inch whole-wheat pita bread, cut or torn into bite-sized pieces

Directions

1. Preheat the over to 400 degrees F.
2. On a large baking sheet, spread torn pita bread and bake for 6 minutes.
3. With the back of a knife, mash garlic and salt until paste-like. Add to a medium bowl.
4. Whisk in ground cumin, and lemon juice. In a steady and slow stream, pour oil as you whisk continuously. Season with pepper.
5. In a large salad bowl, mix cucumber, tomatoes, and beans. Pour in dressing, and toss to coat well.
6. Add mint, parsley, feta, lettuce, and toasted pita, toss to mix once again, and serve.

Nutrition: Calories: 241; Fats: 11.7 g; Carbohydrates: 22.4 g; Protein: 11.4 g

Tomato and Cucumber Salad with Feta

10 minutes

0 minutes

4

Ingredients

- 2 tomatoes
- 1/2 cucumber
- 1/2 bunch of spring onions
- 200 g of feta
- 6 tablespoons of olive oil
- 3 tablespoons of balsamic vinegar
- Salt and pepper

Directions

1. Thoroughly clean the tomatoes and cucumber.
2. Quarter each tomato, cut the cucumber into thin slices and cut the spring onion into thin rings.
3. Chop the herbs and dice the feta.
4. Put all ingredients in a salad bowl. Add oil and balsamic vinegar, season with salt and pepper, and mix well. Done! Serve and enjoy.

Nutrition: Calories: 258; Fats: 22.9 g; Carbohydrates: 4.2 g; Protein: 10.3 g

Mediterranean Salad with Baked Camembert

30 minutes

15 minutes

4

Ingredients

- 800 g of asparagus
- 200 g of rocket
- 200 g of cherry tomatoes
- 100 g of olives
- 3 tablespoons of balsamic vinegar
- 4 mini camembert
- 2 tablespoons of cranberries
- 5 tablespoons of olive oil
- 1 teaspoon of mustard
- Salt and pepper

Directions

1. Clean and peel the asparagus and cut off the woody ends. Cook in boiling salted water for about 10 minutes. Then drain.
2. Thoroughly clean the rocket and spin dry. Wash and quarter the tomatoes.
3. For the dressing: mix the balsamic vinegar, 3 tablespoons of olive oil, salt, mustard, and pepper in a bowl.
4. Bake the Camembert in a preheated oven at 390 degrees F. Then take it out, let it cool and cover with a few cranberries.
5. Arrange the rocket with asparagus, tomatoes, and olives on a plate. Drizzle with the salad dressing and add the melted camembert with cranberries. Finished! Serve and enjoy.

Nutrition: Calories: 232; Fats: 20.1 g; Carbohydrates: 9.2 g; Protein: 4.4 g

Mediterranean Salad with Peppers and Tomatoes

35 minutes

30 minutes

2

Ingredients

- 1 eggplant
- 1 zucchini
- 1 bell pepper
- 4 tomatoes
- 1 onion
- 4 sprigs of rosemary
- 6 sprigs of thyme
- 4 stalks of sage
- 3 tablespoons of olive oil
- 3 tablespoons of balsamic vinegar
- Salt and pepper

Directions

1. Preheat the oven to 390 degrees F.
2. Quarter tomatoes. Cut the remaining vegetables into bite-sized pieces, halve the onion and chop it into small pieces.
3. Line a baking sheet with parchment paper, add the vegetables on top, drizzle with olive oil and mix well.
4. Season with salt and pepper and scatter the herbs over the vegetables. Put the vegetables in the oven and bake for about 30 minutes.
5. Remove and transfer to a large bowl and mix the olive oil with balsamic vinegar. Season with salt and pepper.
6. Let it cool, covered. When the salad is still lukewarm, add the tomato quarters and mix well.
7. Serve the salad lukewarm.

Nutrition: Calories: 245; Fats: 16.4 g; Carbohydrates: 23.8 g; Protein: 2.5 g

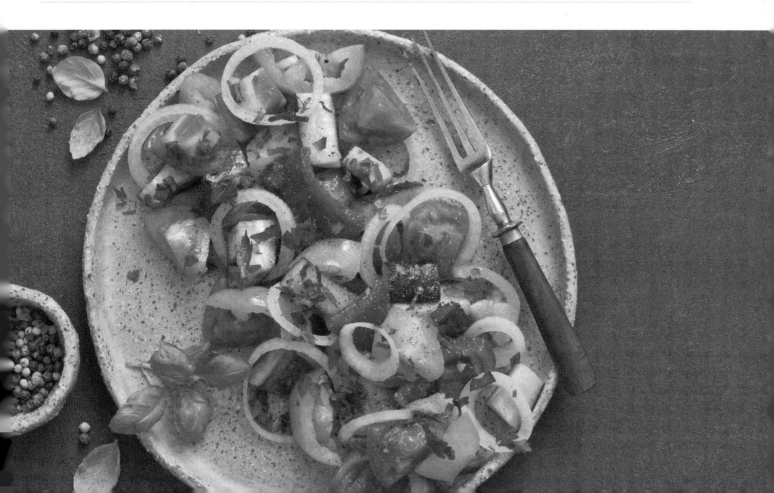

Mediterranean Potato Salad with Beans

180 minutes

15 minutes

4

Ingredients

- 500 g of potatoes
- 300 g of green beans
- 1 tablespoon of rosemary
- 8 sun-dried tomatoes
- 40 g bacon
- 3 tablespoons of red wine vinegar
- 200 g of olives
- 1 egg yolk
- Salt and pepper

Directions

1. Wash green beans, break into short pieces, and boil in salted water for about 10 minutes, then drain in a colander. Collect some boiled bean water.
2. Drain the sun-dried tomatoes and cut them into small pieces.
3. Collect some of the oil from the tomatoes.
4. Chop the rosemary and cut the bacon into thin strips. Fry bacon with chopped rosemary in olive oil and put the tomato oil in a pan.
5. Pour in the vinegar and the bean water and add the tomato pieces. Heat the potatoes and beans, let them steep, and wait until they have cooled down.
6. Then, drain the potatoes and beans using a sieve and collect the vinegar mixture that they have been in. Mix the potato salad with the olives.
7. Whisk the vinaigrette with egg yolk and then heat gently, stirring constantly, until the sauce thickens. Season with salt and pepper and pour over the salad. Let it steep for an hour. Finished! Serve and enjoy.

Nutrition: Calories: 250; Fats: 12.2 g; Carbohydrates: 29.2 g; Protein: 5.8 g

Orzo Olive Salad

180 minutes

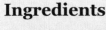

10 minutes

4

Ingredients

- 250 g of orzo
- 100 g of cocktail tomatoes
- 100 g of olives
- Onion
- 1/2 bunch of parsley
- 250 g of feta cheese

FOR THE DRESSING:
- 1 lemon, squeezed
- Salt and pepper
- 30 ml olive oil
- 2 garlic cloves

Directions

1. Cook the pasta for about 10 minutes according to the instructions on the packet. Wash and halve cocktail tomatoes, core the olives, peel and chop the onion, and crumble the feta.
2. For the dressing: mix together the lemon juice, olive oil, garlic, salt, and pepper.
3. Mix the Orzo with the dressing and finally add the remaining ingredients. Serve and enjoy.

Nutrition: Calories: 412; Fats: 22.6 g; Carbohydrates: 33.7 g; Protein: 18.3 g

Mushroom Arugula Salad

25 minutes

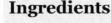

0 minutes

4

Ingredients

- 500 g of mushrooms
- 200 g of sheep cheese
- 75 g of rocket
- 60 g of pine nuts
- 3 tablespoons of olive oil
- Salt and pepper

Directions

1. Wash the mushrooms and cut them into thin slices. Clean the rocket and cut into small pieces. Dice the sheep's cheese.
2. Put everything in a salad bowl with olive oil and balsamic vinegar. Season to taste with salt and pepper.
3. Toast the pine nuts in a pan until they are golden brown.
4. Add the pine nuts to the salad. Serve and enjoy.

Nutrition: Calories: 292; Fats: 20.2 g; Carbohydrates: 13.6 g; Protein: 13.4 g

Shrimp in Lemon Sauce

10 minutes

15 minutes

4

Ingredients

- 1 pound of shrimp, peeled and deveined
- 1/3 cup of lemon juice
- 4 egg yolks
- 2 tablespoons of olive oil
- 1 cup of chicken stock
- Salt and black pepper to taste
- 1 cup of black olives, pitted and halved
- 1 tablespoon thyme, chopped

Directions

1. In a bowl, mix the lemon juice with the egg yolks and whisk well.
2. Heat the oil in a pan over medium heat, add the shrimp and cook for 2 minutes on each side and transfer to a plate.
3. Heat the stock in a separate pan over medium heat. Add some of this over the egg yolks and lemon juice mix and whisk well.
4. Add this to the rest of the stock. Also add salt and pepper, whisk well and simmer for 2 minutes.
5. Add the shrimp and the rest of the ingredients, toss and serve right away.

Nutrition: Calories: 168; Fats: 14.3 g; Carbohydrates: 1.4 g; Protein: 10.6 g

---

Shrimp and Beans Salad

123

10 minutes

4 minutes

4

Ingredients

- 1 pound of shrimp, peeled and deveined
- 30 ounces of canned cannellini beans, drained and rinsed
- 2 tablespoons of olive oil
- 1 cup of cherry tomatoes, halved
- 1 teaspoon of lemon zest, grated
- 1/2 cup of red onion, chopped
- A pinch of salt and black pepper

FOR THE DRESSING:
- 3 tablespoons of red wine vinegar
- 2 garlic cloves, minced
- 1/2 cup of olive oil

Directions

1. Heat the 2 tablespoons of oil in a pan over medium-high heat.
2. Add the shrimp and cook for 2 minutes on each side.
3. In a salad bowl, combine the shrimp with the beans, and the rest of the ingredients except for the ones for the dressing, and toss.
4. In a separate bowl, combine the vinegar with 1/2 cup of oil and the garlic and whisk well.
5. Pour over the salad, toss, and serve right away.

Nutrition: Calories: 436; Fats: 16.3 g; Carbohydrates: 42.4 g; Protein: 28.7 g

Chicken Tortillas

60 minutes

15 minutes

4

Ingredients

- 1/2 cup of mayonnaise
- 1 finely minced small garlic clove
- 8-ounce chopped unsalted cooked chicken
- 1/2 of seeded and chopped red bell pepper
- 1/2 of seeded and chopped green bell pepper
- 1 chopped red onion
- 4 (6-ounce) warmed corn tortillas

Directions

1. In a bowl, mix mayonnaise and garlic.
2. In another bowl, mix chicken and vegetables.
3. Arrange the tortillas on a smooth surface.
4. Spread the mayonnaise mixture over each tortilla evenly.
5. Put the chicken mixture over 1/4 of each tortilla.
6. Fold the outside edges inward and roll up like a burrito.
7. Secure each tortilla with toothpicks to secure the filling.
8. Cut each tortilla in half and serve.

Nutrition: Calories: 261; Fats: 8.2 g; Carbohydrates: 34.3 g; Protein: 13.5 g

Chicken Nuggets with Honey Mustard Dipping Sauce

51 minutes

20 minutes

3

Ingredients

- 1 tablespoon of mustard, yellow
- 1/2 cup of mayonnaise
- 1/3 cup of honey
- 2 teaspoons of Worcestershire sauce
- 1 egg (large)
- 2 tablespoons of milk with a fat content of 1%
- 3 cups of cornflakes
- 1 pound of boneless chicken breast.

Directions

1. In a medium bowl, combine the mustard, mayonnaise and honey, as well as Worcestershire sauce. Chill the sauce unless the nuggets are done, then use as a condiment.
2. Preheat the oven to 400 degrees F.
3. The chicken breast should be cut into 36 bite-sized chunks.
4. Cornflakes should be crushed and poured into a big zip-lock bag.
5. In a medium bowl, whisk together the beaten egg and milk.
6. After dipping the chicken pieces in the mixture of eggs, shake them in a zip-lock bag to cover them with the cornflake crumbs.
7. Bake nuggets for about 15 minutes on a baking tray coated with nonstick baking spray.

Nutrition: Calories: 316; Fats: 12.7 g; Carbohydrates: 18.3 g; Protein: 32.3 g

Chapter 5
Desserts

Peaches Poached in Rose Water

10 minutes

20 minutes

6

Ingredients

- 1 cup of water
- 1 cup of rose water
- 1/4 cup of wildflower honey
- 8 green cardamom pods, lightly crushed
- 1 teaspoon vanilla bean paste
- 6 large yellow peaches, pitted and quartered
- 1/2 cup of chopped unsalted roasted pistachio meats

Directions

1. Add water, rose water, honey, cardamom, and vanilla to a pan. Gently heat until the honey has dissolved.
2. Add peaches. Close the lid and simmer gently for 15 minutes but occasionally turning them and covering them with the liquid.
3. Allow the peaches to stand for 10 minutes. Carefully remove peaches from the poaching liquid with a slotted spoon.
4. Slip the skins from the peach slices. Arrange the slices on a plate and garnish with pistachios. Serve warm or at room temperature.

Nutrition: Calories: 106; Fats: 2.8 g; Carbohydrates: 19.2 g; Protein: 1.2 g

Poached Apples with Greek Yogurt and Granola

5 minutes

15 minutes

4

Ingredients

- 4 medium-sized apples, peeled
- 1/2 cup of brown sugar
- 1 vanilla bean
- 1 cinnamon stick
- 1/2 cup of cranberry juice
- 1 cup of water
- 1/2 cup of 2% Greek yogurt
- 1/2 cup of granola

Directions

1. Add the apples, brown sugar, water, cranberry juice, vanilla bean, and cinnamon stick to a pressure cooker.
2. Secure the lid and cook for 5 minutes at high pressure. Once cooking is complete, use a natural pressure release for 5 minutes; carefully remove the lid.
3. Put the poached apples to one side and transfer the liquid to a saute pan. Heat gently until it has thickened.
4. Add the apples to serving bowls. Add the syrup and top each apple with granola and Greek yogurt. Enjoy!

Nutrition: Calories: 169; Fats: 2.1 g; Carbohydrates: 33.3 g; Protein: 4.5 g

Healthy Avocado Chocolate Pudding

5 minutes

0 minutes

4

Ingredients

- 6 avocados, peeled, pitted, and cut into chunks
- 1/2 cup of pure maple syrup, or more to taste
- 3/4 cup of unsweetened cocoa powder
- 2 teaspoons of vanilla extract
- Fresh mint leaves, optional

Directions

1. In a food processor, purée the avocados, maple syrup, cocoa powder, and vanilla until smooth.
2. Garnish with mint leaves, if desired.
3. Ingredient Tip: Avoid leftovers and eat it all! The avocado will oxidize and turn brown after just a few hours.

Nutrition: Calories: 422; Fats: 35.2 g; Carbohydrates: 20.8 g; Protein: 6.8 g

Classic Chocolate Mousse

15 minutes

0 minutes

4

Ingredients

- 8 ounces of bittersweet or semisweet vegan chocolate
- 1 3/4 cups of (about 1 pound) silken tofu
- 1/2 cup of pure maple syrup
- 1 teaspoon vanilla
- 1 1/2 teaspoons of ground cinnamon

Directions

1. Create a double boiler by bringing a medium pot filled halfway with water to a low simmer.
2. Add a heatproof bowl above the water and make sure it is not touching the water. Add the chocolate to the bowl. Keep the pot over low heat and stir the chocolate until it is melted and silky smooth.
3. In a food processor, add all the ingredients. Blend until smooth.
4. Place the mousse in a bowl and refrigerate before serving.
5. Substitution Tip: Substitute 1 teaspoon of chili powder for the ground cinnamon

Nutrition: Calories: 248; Fats: 13.8 g; Carbohydrates: 20.3 g; Protein: 10.8 g

Banana Ice Cream with Chocolate Sauce

10 minutes

0 minutes

4

Ingredients

- 1/2 cup of raw unsalted cashews
- 1/4 cup of pure maple syrup
- 1 tablespoon unsweetened cocoa powder
- 1 teaspoon vanilla extract
- 1/4 teaspoon salt
- 1/4 cup of water
- 6 ripe bananas, peeled and frozen

Directions

1. Put cashews in a bowl and add water. Soak cashews for two hours or overnight. Drain and rinse.
2. In a food processor or blender, add the cashews, maple syrup, cocoa powder, vanilla, and salt. Blend, adding the water a couple of tablespoons at a time until you get a smooth consistency.
3. Transfer to an airtight container, then refrigerate. Bring to room temperature before using.
4. Add frozen bananas to the food processor. Process until you have smooth banana ice cream. Serve topped with chocolate sauce.
5. Ingredient tip: The best way to freeze a banana is to start with ripe peeled bananas. Slice them into 2-inch chunks and arrange them in a single layer on a parchment-lined baking sheet. Pop them in the freezer. Once frozen, transfer to freezer-safe bags. Frozen bananas are also a delicious, healthy addition to smoothies. Individually freeze chunks of one banana, and you'll always be ready to create an icy, rich, creamy smoothie.

Nutrition: Calories: 258; Fats: 10.4 g; Carbohydrates: 37.5 g; Protein: 3.5 g

Raspberry Lime Sorbet

**15 minutes, plus
5 hours or more
to chill**

0 minutes

4

Ingredients

- 3 pints of fresh raspberries or 2 (10-ounce) bags of frozen
- 1/2 cup of fresh orange juice
- 4 tablespoons of pure maple syrup
- 3 tablespoons of fresh lime juice
- Dark chocolate curls, optional

Directions

1. In a glass dish, combine the raspberries, orange juice, maple syrup, and lime juice. Stir well to mix. Cover then put it in the freezer until frozen solid, about 5 hours.
2. Get it from the freezer and let it sit for 10 minutes. Crush chunks with a knife or large spoon and transfer the mixture to a food processor. Process this until smooth and creamy for 5 minutes. Serve immediately. The sorbet will freeze solid again, but can be processed again until creamy just before serving.
3. To serve, add a scoop into an ice cream dish. Garnish with fresh raspberries and dark chocolate curls, if using.
4. Preparation Tip: To make chocolate curls, use a vegetable peeler, and scrape the blade lengthwise across a piece of solid chocolate to create pretty, delicate curls. Refrigerate the curls until ready to use.

Nutrition: Calories: 68; Fats: 0 g; Carbohydrates: 16.3 g; Protein: 0.8 g

Baked Apples with Dried Fruit

10 minutes

1 hour

4

Ingredients

- 4 large apples, cored to make a cavity
- 4 teaspoons of raisins or cranberries
- 4 teaspoons of pure maple syrup
- 1/2 teaspoon ground cinnamon
- 1/2 cup of unsweetened apple juice or water

Directions

1. Preheat the oven to 350 degrees F.
2. Add apples in a baking pan that will hold them upright. Put the dried fruit into the cavities and drizzle with maple syrup. Sprinkle with cinnamon. Pour apple juice or water on the apples.
3. Cover loosely with foil and bake for 50 minutes to 1 hour, or until the apples are tender when pierced with a fork.
4. Serving Suggestion: Serve the apples topped with Vegan Whipped Cream.

Nutrition: Calories: 87; Fats: 1 g; Carbohydrates: 21.3 g; Protein: 1 g

Jasmine Rice Pudding with Cranberries

5 minutes

15 minutes

4

Ingredients

- 1 cup of apple juice
- 1 heaped tablespoon of honey
- 1/3 cup of granulated sugar
- 1 1/2 cup of jasmine rice
- 1 cup of water
- 1/4 teaspoon of ground cinnamon
- 1/4 teaspoon of ground cloves
- 1/3 teaspoon of ground cardamom
- 1 teaspoon of vanilla extract
- 3 eggs, well-beaten
- 1/2 cup of cranberries

Directions

1. Thoroughly combine the apple juice, honey, sugar, jasmine rice, water, and spices to a pressure cooker and cook for 4 minutes at high pressure.
2. Once cooking is complete, use natural pressure release for 5 minutes; then carefully remove the lid.
3. Fold in the eggs while the pudding is hot.
4. Ladle into individual bowls and top with dried cranberries. Enjoy!

Nutrition: Calories: 237; Fats: 2.6 g; Carbohydrates: 46.1 g; Protein: 8.3 g

Cardamom Date Bites

15 minutes, plus time to soak

15 minutes

8

Ingredients

- 1 cup of pitted dates
- 3 cups of old-fashioned rolled oats
- 1/4 cup of ground flaxseed
- 1 teaspoon ground cardamom
- 3 ripe bananas, mashed (about 1 1/2 cup)

Directions

1. Preheat the oven to 350 degrees F. Line a baking sheet with parchment paper.
2. In a small bowl, add the dates and cover them with hot water. Let it sit until softened, 10 to 30 minutes, depending on the dates, and then drain. Purée in a food processor or blender. Set the date paste aside.
3. In a food processor, grind the oats and ground flaxseed until they resemble flour.
4. In a large bowl, mix together the cardamom and mashed bananas. Stir in the ground oat-flaxseed mixture.
5. Form into walnut-size balls and flatten a little. Add to the baking sheet and form an indentation in the middle using a 1/4 teaspoon measuring spoon. Fill each indentation with about 1/2 teaspoon of date paste.
6. Bake for 15 minutes or until the bites are golden.

Nutrition: Calories: 151; Fats: 1.9 g; Carbohydrates: 28.8 g; Protein: 5.1 g

Vegan Chocolate Mousse

15 minutes

0 minutes

4

Ingredients

- 8 ounces of bittersweet or semisweet vegan chocolate
- 1 3/4 cups of (about 1 pound) silken tofu
- 1/2 cup of pure maple syrup
- 1 teaspoon vanilla
- 1 1/2 teaspoons of ground cinnamon

Directions

1. Create a double boiler by bringing a medium pot filled halfway with water to a low simmer. Place a heatproof bowl above and make sure it is not touching the water. Add the chocolate to the bowl. Keep the pot over low heat and stir the chocolate until it is melted and silky smooth.
2. In a food processor, add all the ingredients. Blend until smooth.
3. Refrigerate before serving.

Nutrition: Calories: 248; Fat: 13.8 g; Carbs: 20.3 g; Protein: 10.8 g

Moroccan Stuffed Dates

15 minutes

0 minute

30

Ingredients

- 1 pound of dates
- 1 cup of blanched almonds
- 1/4 cup of sugar
- 1 1/2 tablespoon of orange flower water
- 1 tablespoon of butter, melted
- 1/4 teaspoon cinnamon

Directions

1. Process the almonds, sugar, and cinnamon in a food processor.
2. Add the butter and orange flower water and process until a smooth paste is formed.
3. Roll small pieces of almond paste the same length as a date.
4. Take a date, make a vertical cut and discard the pit. Insert a piece of the almond paste and press the sides of the date firmly around.
5. Repeat with all the remaining dates and almond paste.

Nutrition: Calories: 51; Fats: 1.3 g; Carbohydrates: 9.3 g; Protein: 0.3 g

Chapter 6
21 Days Meal Plan

	Breakfast	**Lunch**	**Dinner**
1	Walnut & Date Smoothie	Chicken Tortillas	Beef Hash with Zucchini
2	The Great Barley Porridge	Marinated Tuna Steak	Mediterranean Pasta with Tomato Sauce and Vegetables
3	Orange French Toast	Mediterranean Chickpea Salad	Pan-Fried Pork Chops with Orange Sauce
4	Zucchini Muffins	Turkey and Asparagus Mix	Paprika Butter Shrimps with side salad
5	Cardamom-Cinnamon Overnight Oats	Bean and Toasted Pita Salad	Charred Sirloin with Creamy Horseradish Sauce
6	Strawberry Rhubarb Smoothie	Mediterranean Salad with Baked Camembert	Chargrilled Mediterranean Vegetable and Beef Lasagna
7	Baked Dandelion Toast	Greek Turkey Burger	Pasta Bolognese
8	Vanilla Raspberry Overnight Oats	Tomato and Cucumber Salad with Feta	Kataifi-Wrapped Shrimp with Lemon-Garlic Butter
9	Cool Tomato and Dill Frittata	Cod with Grapes, Pecans, Fennel & Kale	Sausage Stuffed Mushrooms
10	Gingerbread & Pumpkin Smoothie	Mediterranean Potato Salad with Beans	Mediterranean Chili Beef
11	Cheesy Egg Muffins	Orzo Olive Salad	Calamari with Tomato Sauce
12	Walnut & Date Smoothie	Halibut Roulade	Italian Pork Loin
13	Caprese Omelet	Chorizo-Kidney Beans Quinoa Pilaf	Easy Fall-Off-the-Bone Ribs

14	Cardamom-Cinnamon Overnight Oats	Shrimp and Beans Salad	Yogurt Chicken Breasts
15	Orange French Toast	Honey Balsamic Chicken	Vegetable and Red Lentil Stew
16	Caprese Omelet	Asparagus Pasta	Grilled Lamb Gyro Burger
17	The Great Barley Porridge	Mushroom Arugula Salad	Zucchini and Chicken
18	Gingerbread & Pumpkin Smoothie	Chicken Nuggets with Honey Mustard Dipping Sauce	Grilled Seabass with Lemon Butter
19	Quick Spinach & Egg Bake	Grilled Sardines	Mediterranean Tortellini
20	Zucchini Muffins	Turkey Verde with Brown Rice	Mashed Beans with Cumin & Egg Topper
21	Vanilla Raspberry Overnight Oats	Mediterranean Salad with Peppers and Tomatoes	Roasted Lamb with Vegetables

DISCOVER THE AMAZING BONUS I HAVE IN STORE FOR YOU

Scan the QR Code or go to www.vitaminsmineralsguides.com
for instant access to the 2 FREE life-saving guides that come with this Book:

FREE: A PRACTICAL 70+ PAGE GUIDEBOOK

Discover the vitamins and minerals that should never be missing from your diet - and which foods you can get them from-.

A free ultra-detailed report – suitable for beginners too – to discover all the essential nutrients for living a long and healthy life

Here is everything you will find in this guide

» What are vitamins and why are they essential
» Minerals - what they do and why you should never be missing them in your diet-
» The 8 signs that you are deficient in vitamins or minerals and how to remedy that
» 3 facts that (maybe) you won't know about vitamins and minerals
» And much much more...

Printed in Great Britain
by Amazon

16916252R00070